Choosing Joy

Kerrie Woodhouse

To my beautiful children, who are

my greatest source of joy.

Experience the joy of brightening someone's day.

Download a free printable card today to send to someone you care about.

Go on. Make their day.

tiny.cc/gracecard

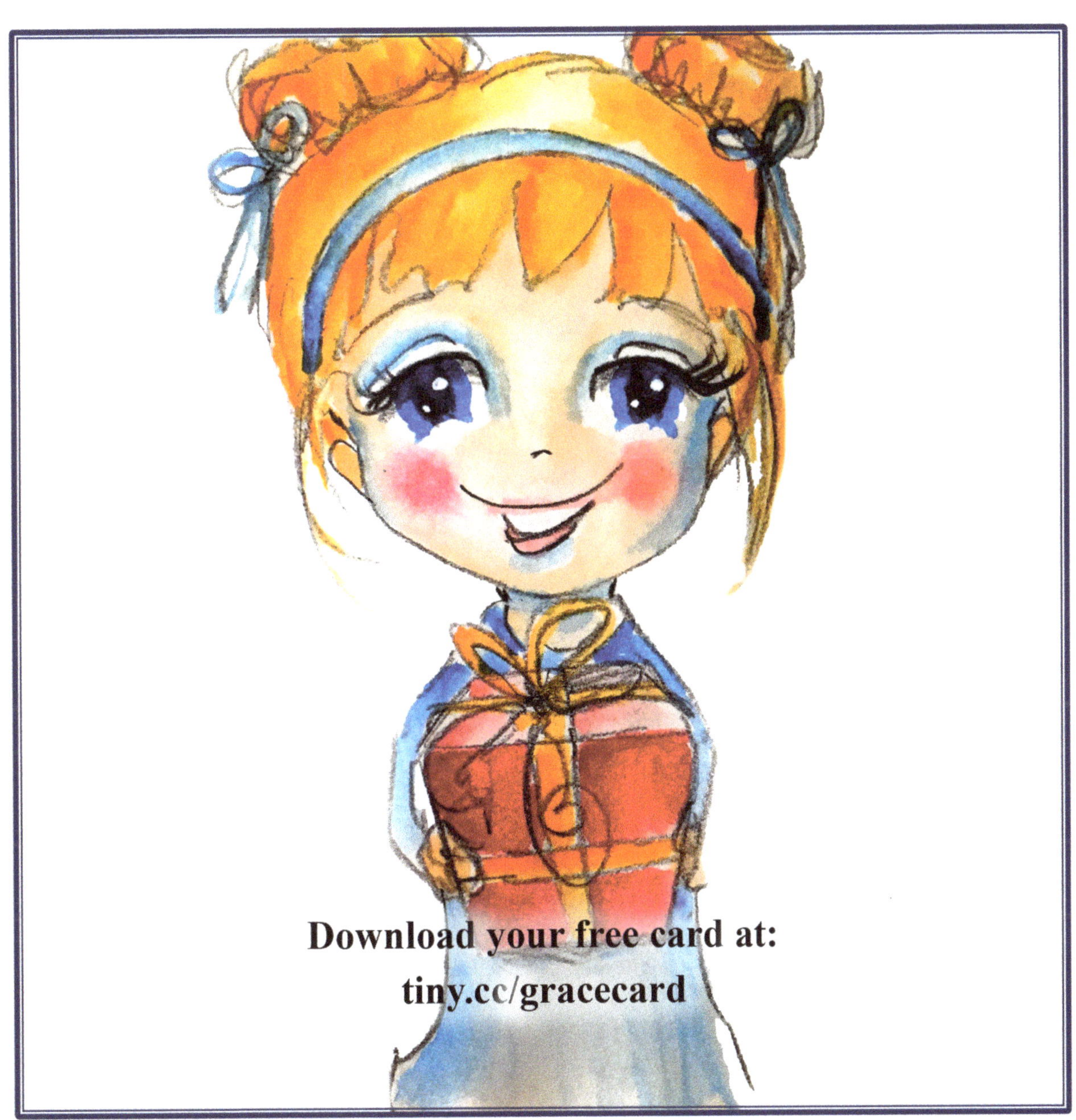
Download your free card at:
tiny.cc/gracecard

Contents

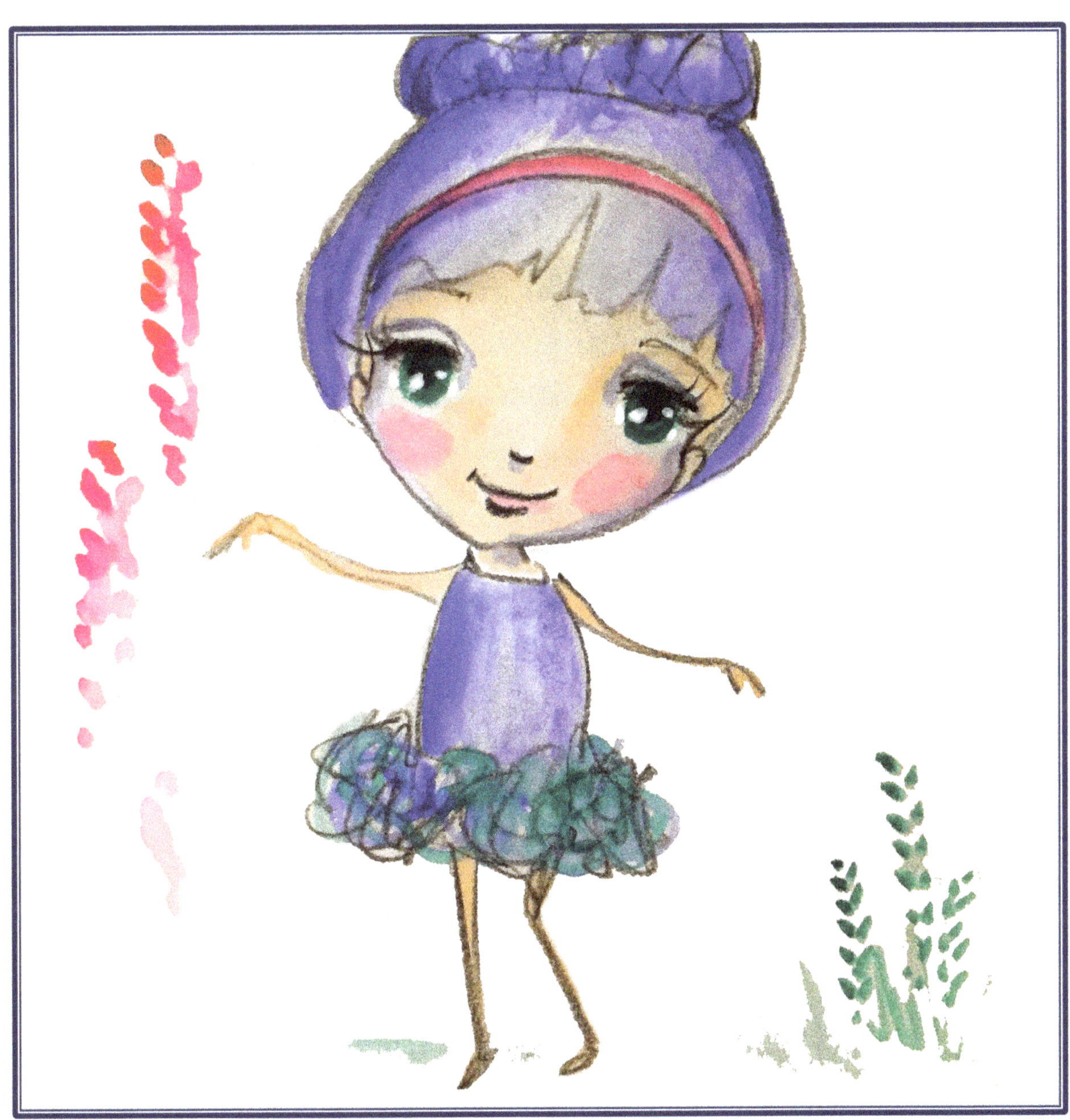

Introduction

The Grace Girls series was born of a small creative project, almost by accident, it seems now.

A daily visit to the sketchbook to complete a small drawing of a whimsical girl. Eventually it became apparent that each girl bore a message.

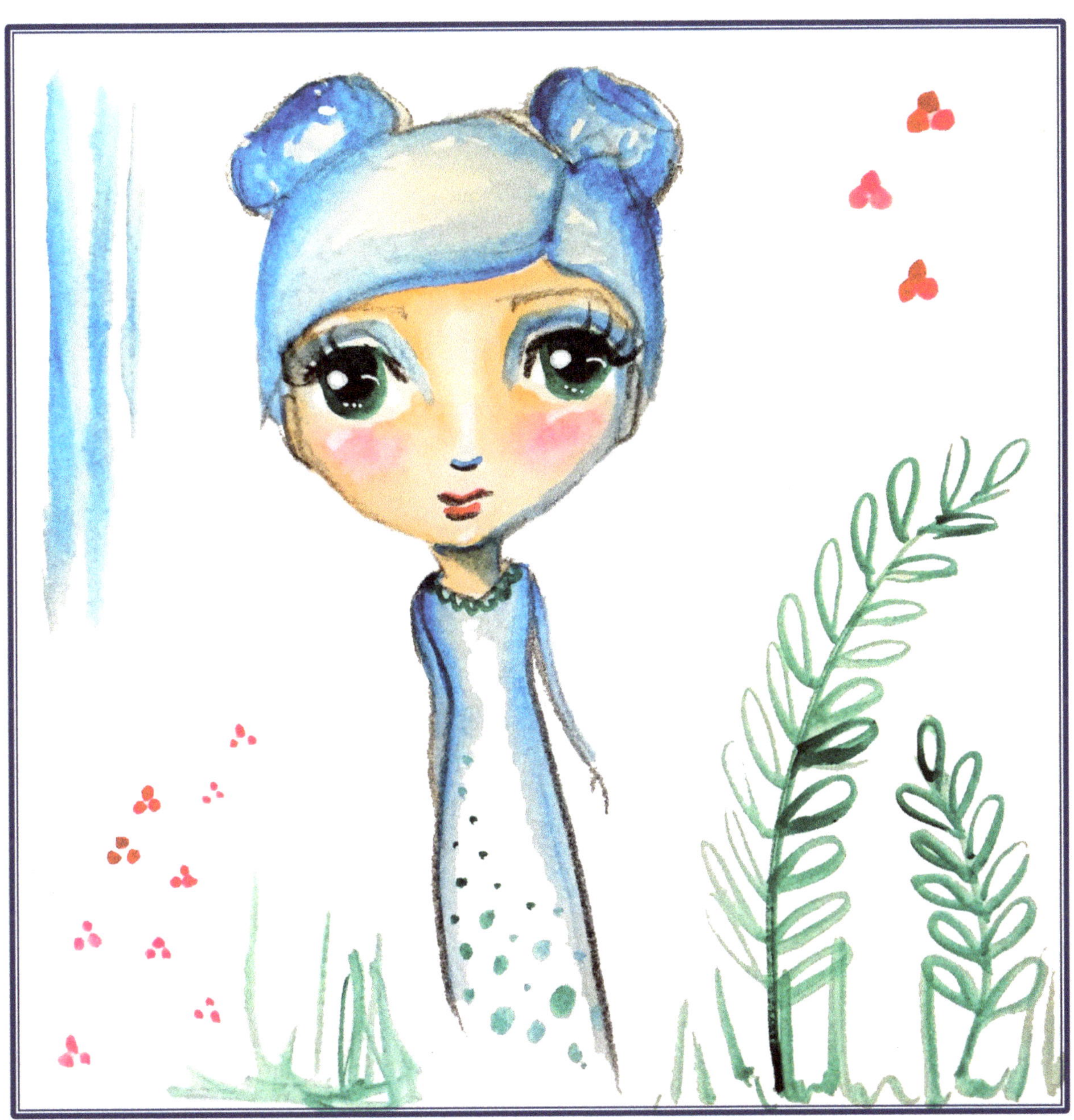

It all started with Grace. She appeared during a period in my life when I was supporting a dear friend through cancer treatment. The first volume in this series, *Finding Grace*, is her story.

Grace's message was one of acceptance. It is only when we accept things just as they are that we can begin to move forward. When we find the grace to accept what we do not have we can begin to find the joy in what we do have.

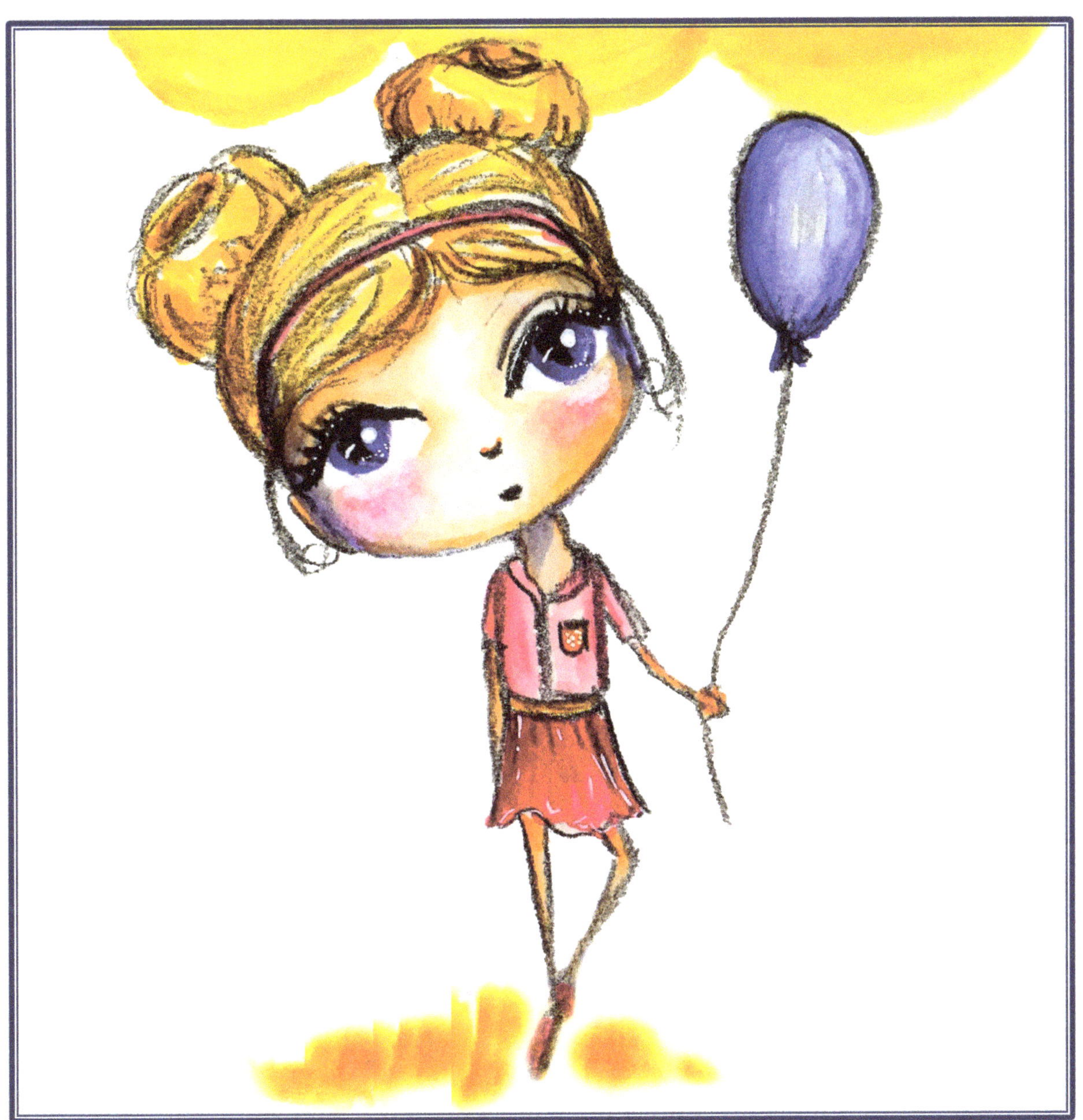

"True happiness is an acceptance of life as it is given to us, with its diminishment, mystery, uncontrollability, and all."

Michael Gellert

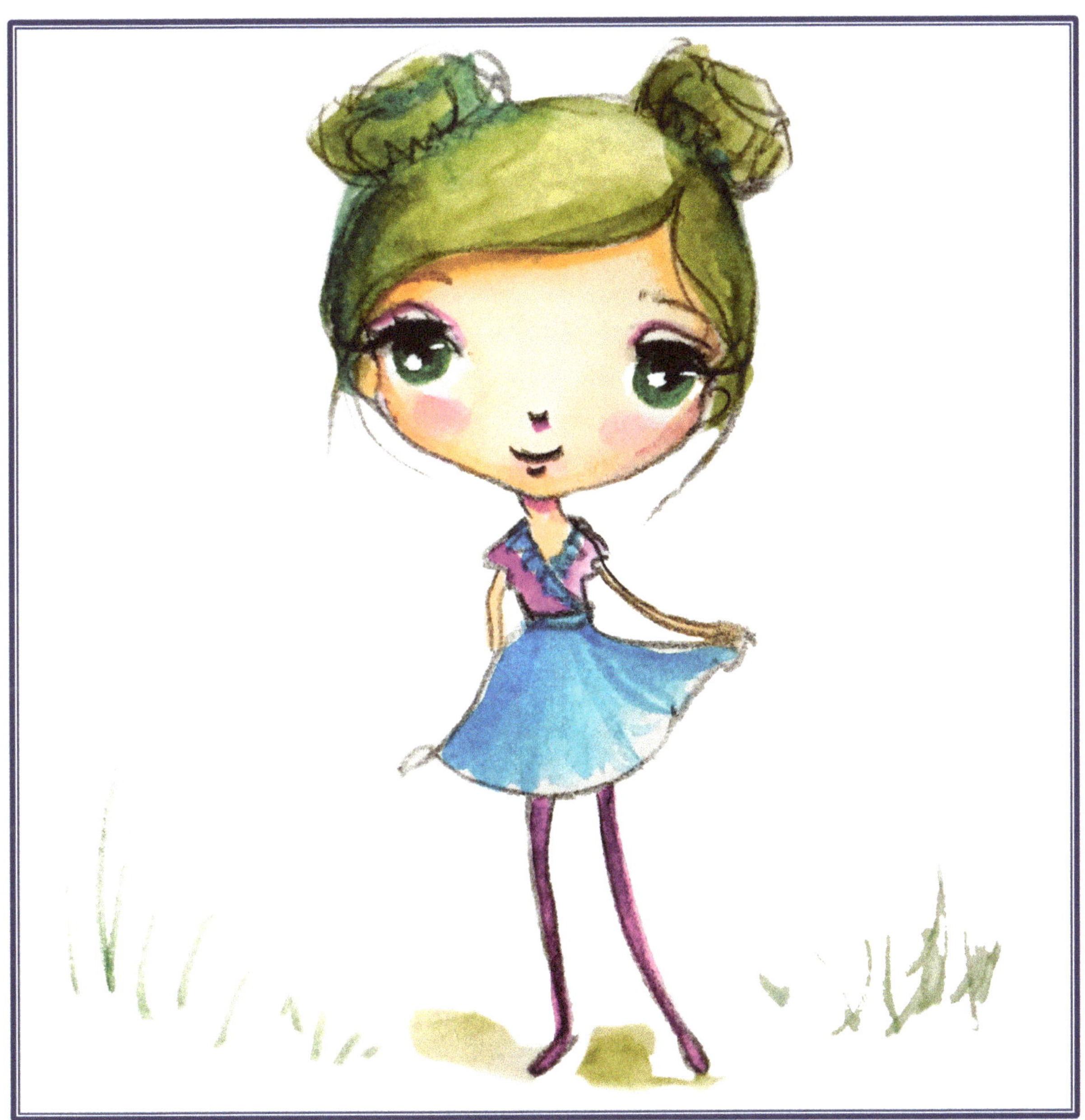

Joy and the rest of the girls in this volume of the series remind us to consistently choose joy. To gather the tiny delights in every day. To make time to pursue that which brings us joy.

For choosing joy is the path to happiness.

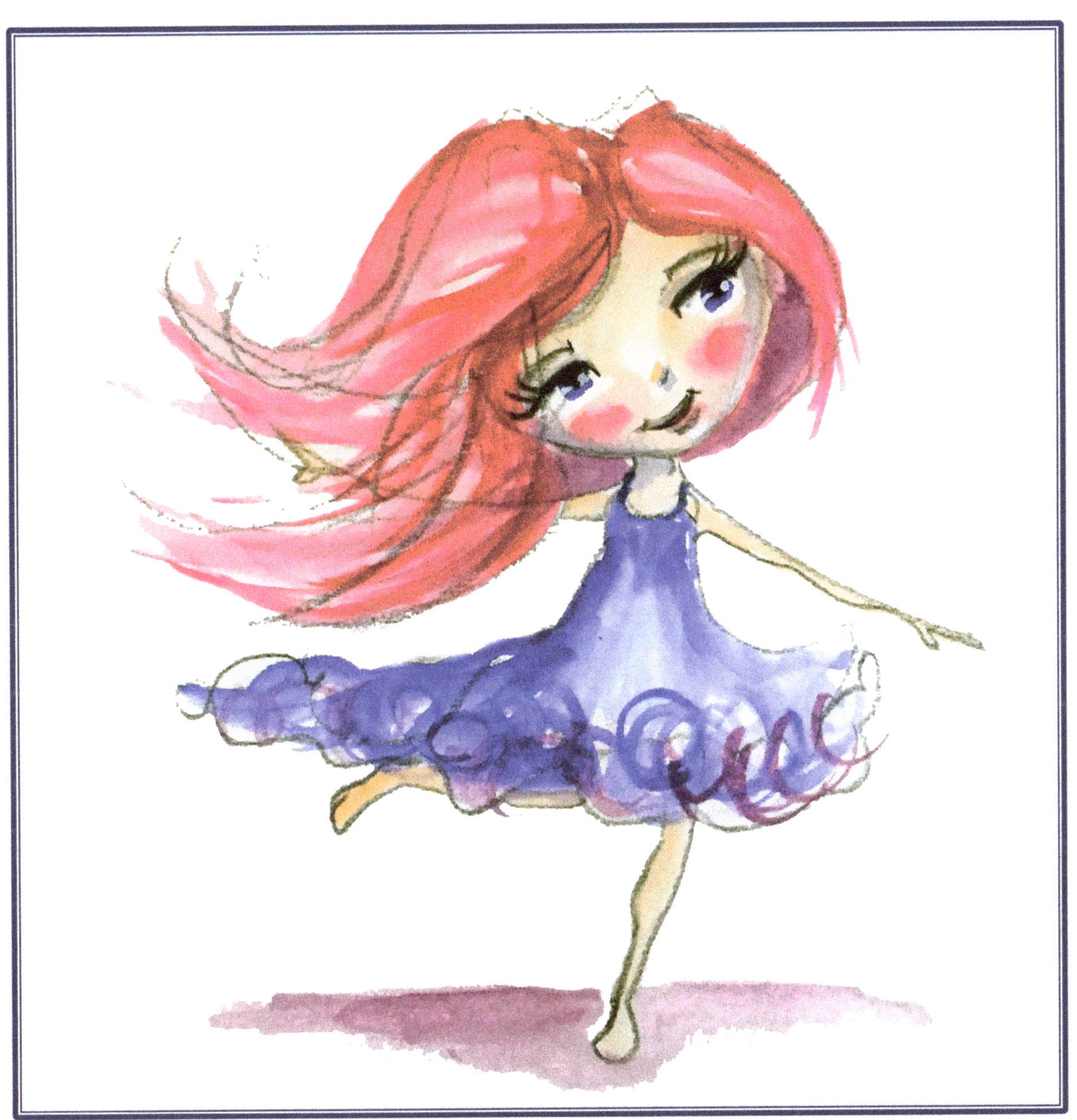

"Happiness is the meaning and the purpose of life, the whole aim and end of human existence."

Aristotle

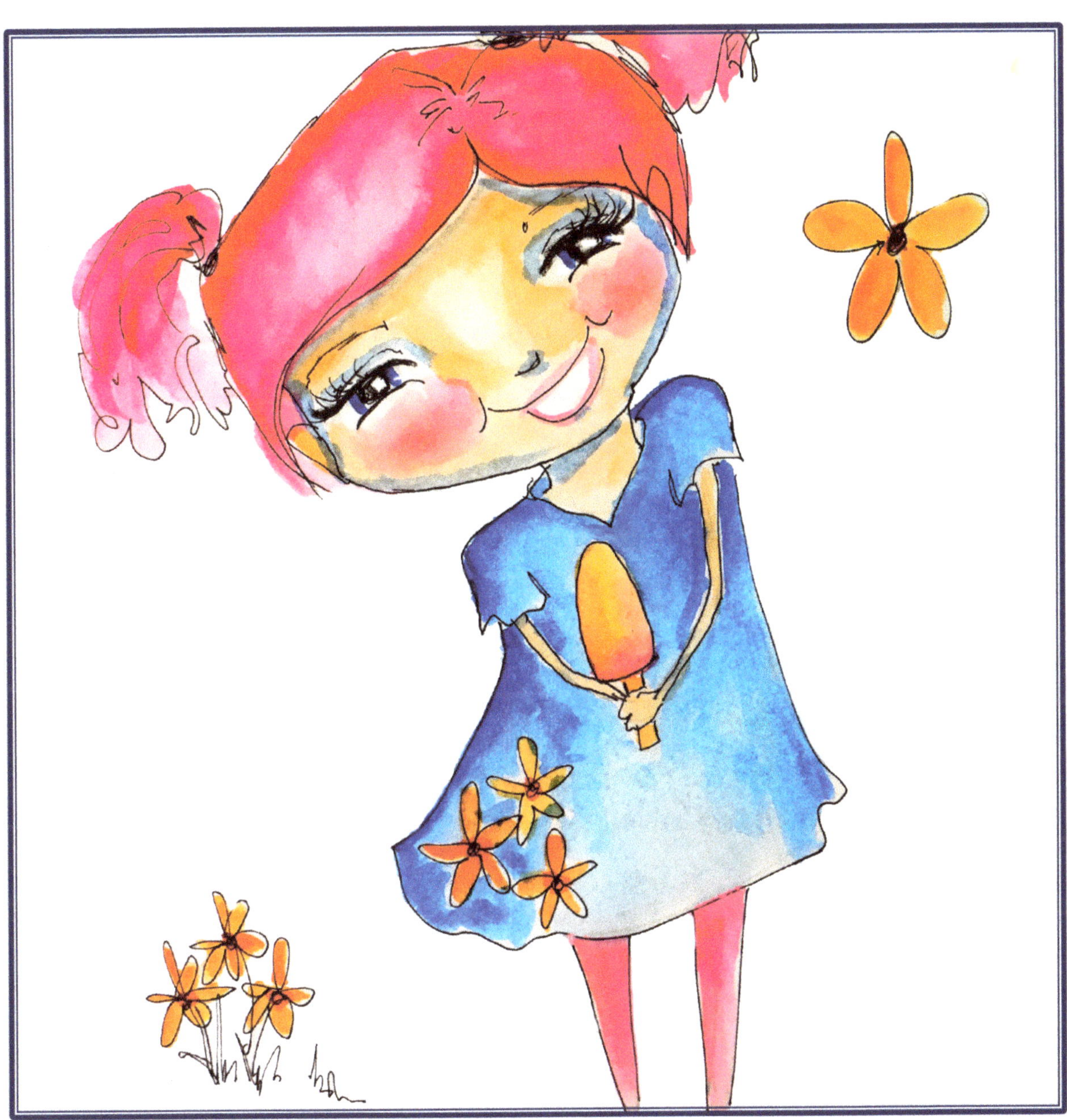

What joy is not

Our lives are complicated tapestries of thoughts experiences and events. Rich and varied. Some of these things are wonderful and glorious. Some are sad, frustrating and difficult. Choosing joy does not mean that we brush a positive varnish over the darker parts of our life. It does not mean we ignore them or pretend they are something they are not.

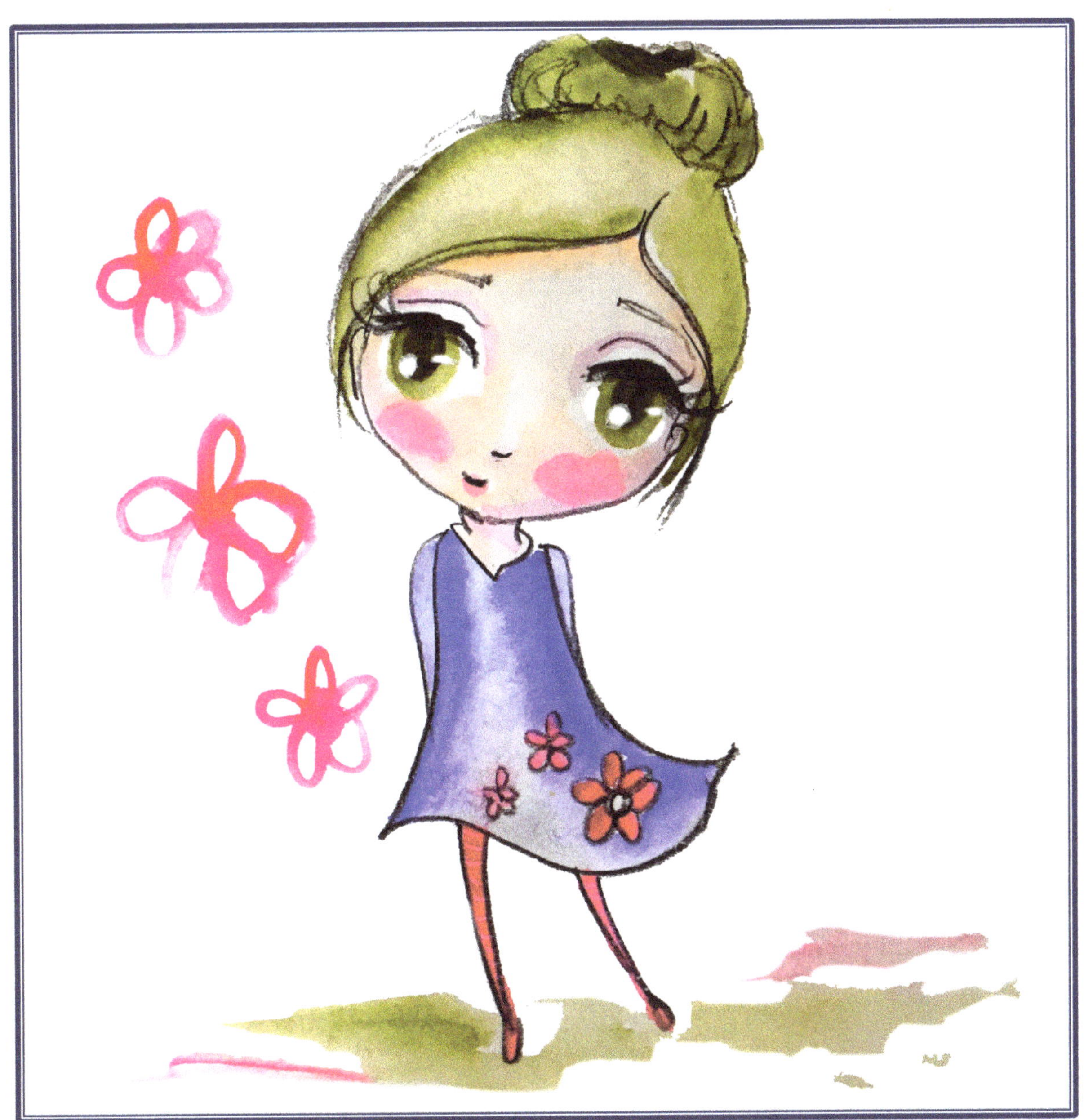

That would diminish our experiences - all of which are valuable. We learn from the difficulties in our lives. They present us with the opportunity to grow. We recognise these challenges, acknowledge them and then choose joy, in spite of the issues. Perhaps because of them.

Without sorrow we might not be able to recognise joy. It is only because of the dark that we can appreciate the light.

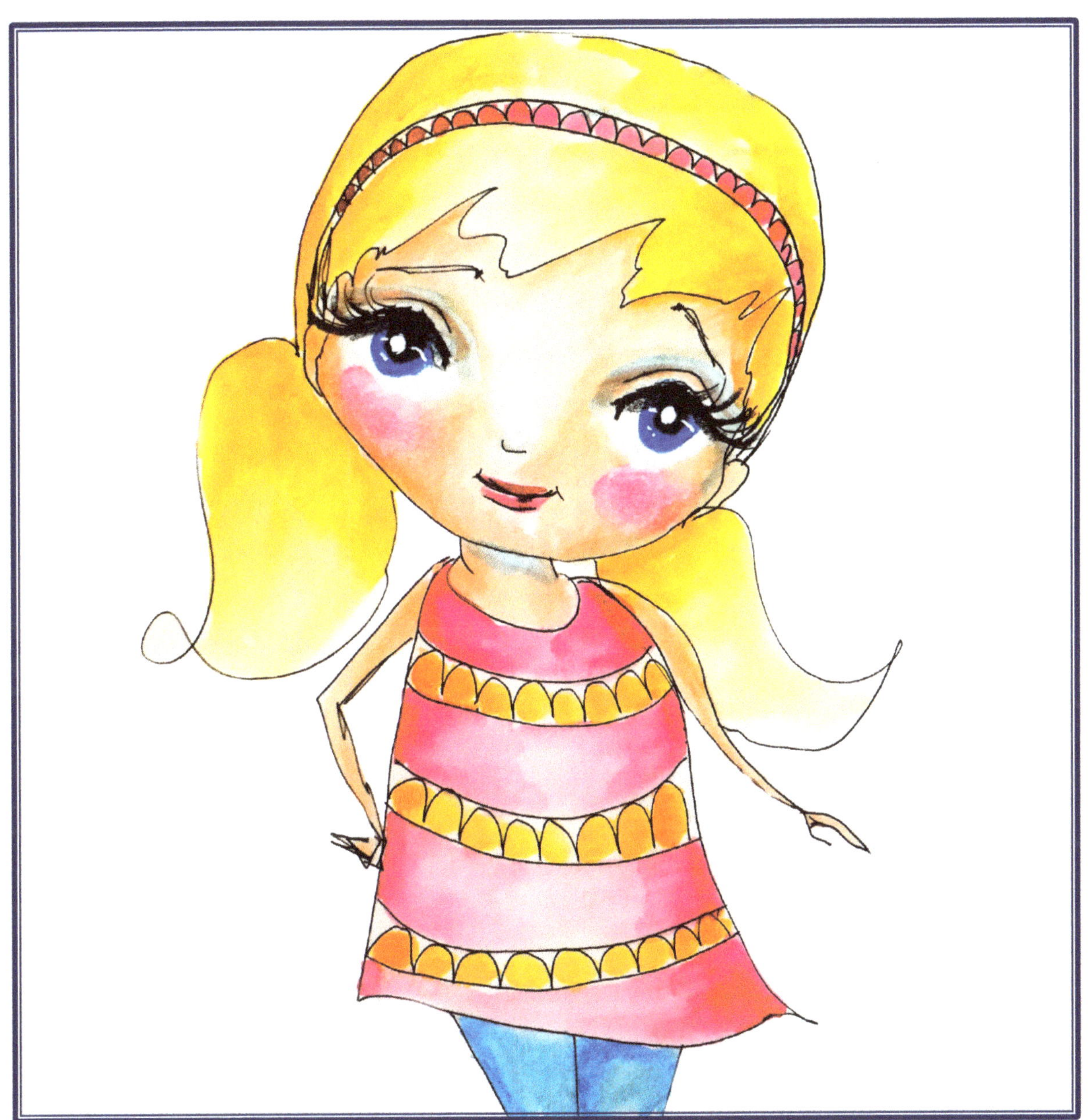

"Your joy is your sorrow unmasked. And the self same well from which your laughter rises was oftentimes filled with your tears…

the deeper that sorrow carves into your being, the more joy you can contain."

Kahlil Gibran

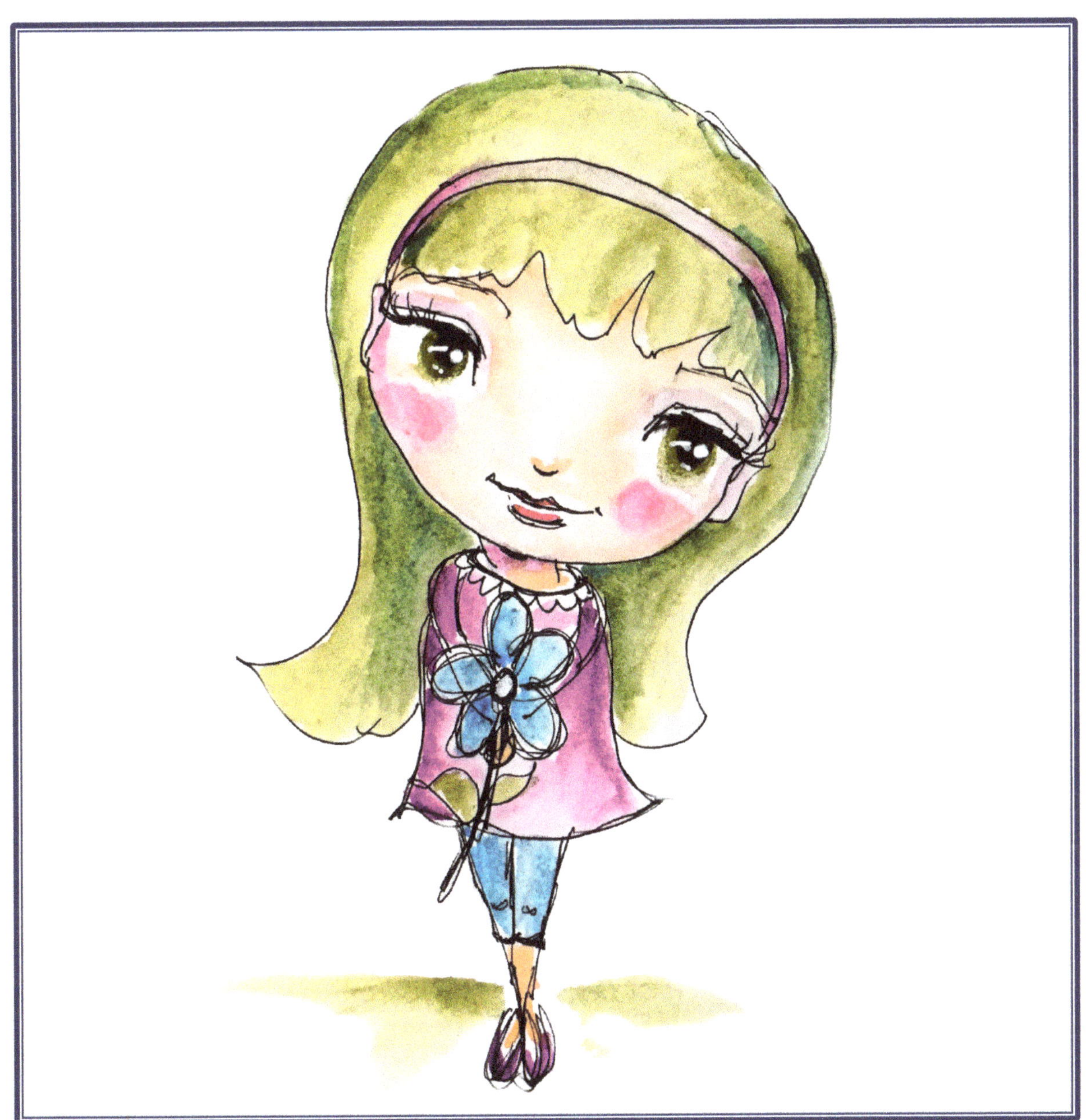

"When you are joyous, look deep into your heart and you shall find it is only that which has given you sorrow that is giving you joy. When you are sorrowful, look again into your heart, and you will see that you are weeping for that which has been your delight."

Kahlil Gibran

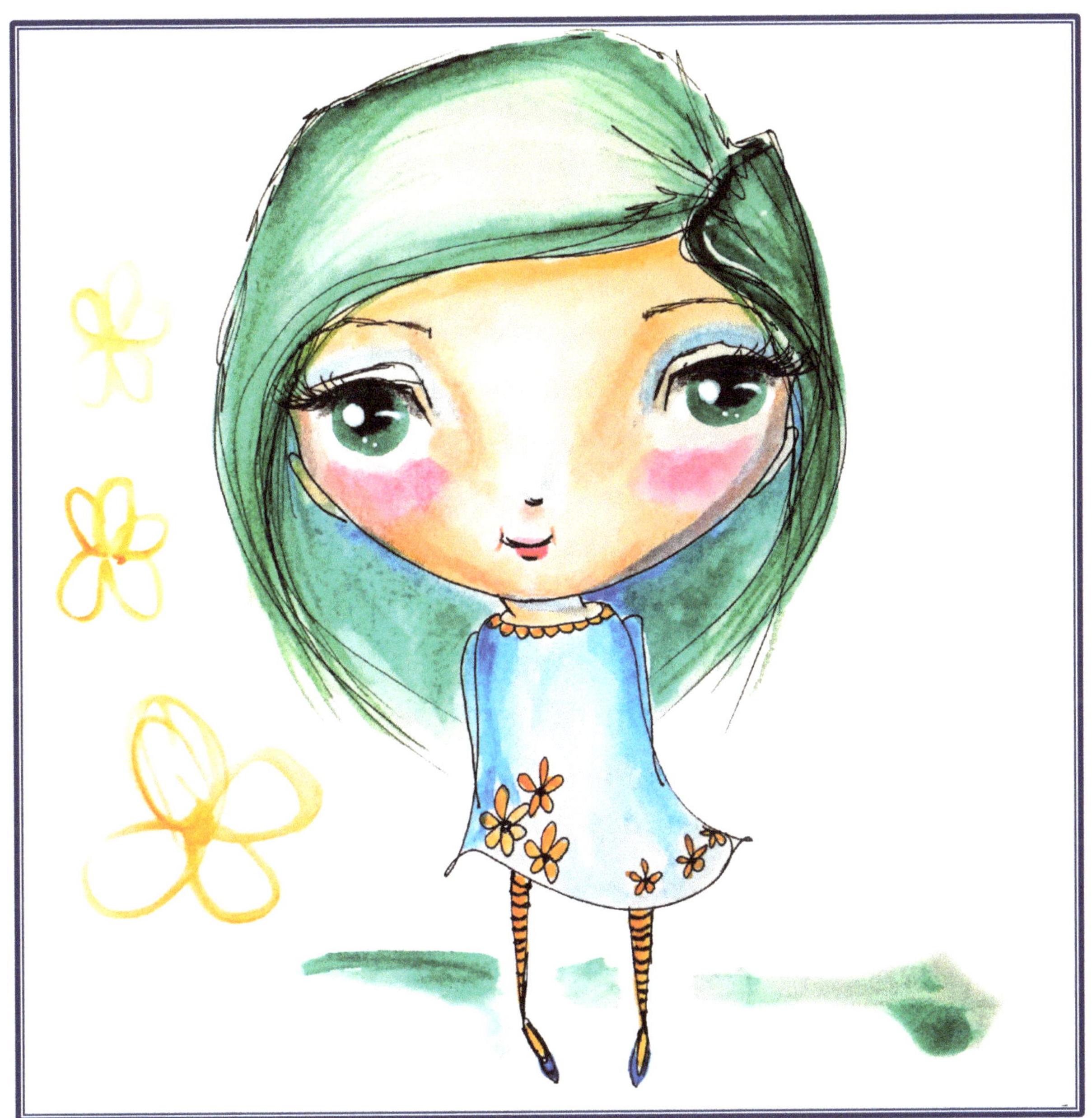

Making a choice

Choosing joy is about finding a balance. The sources of grief and sadness, fear and anger will always exist. They are a part of the world we experience in as much as the joy and happiness, laughter and optimism are.

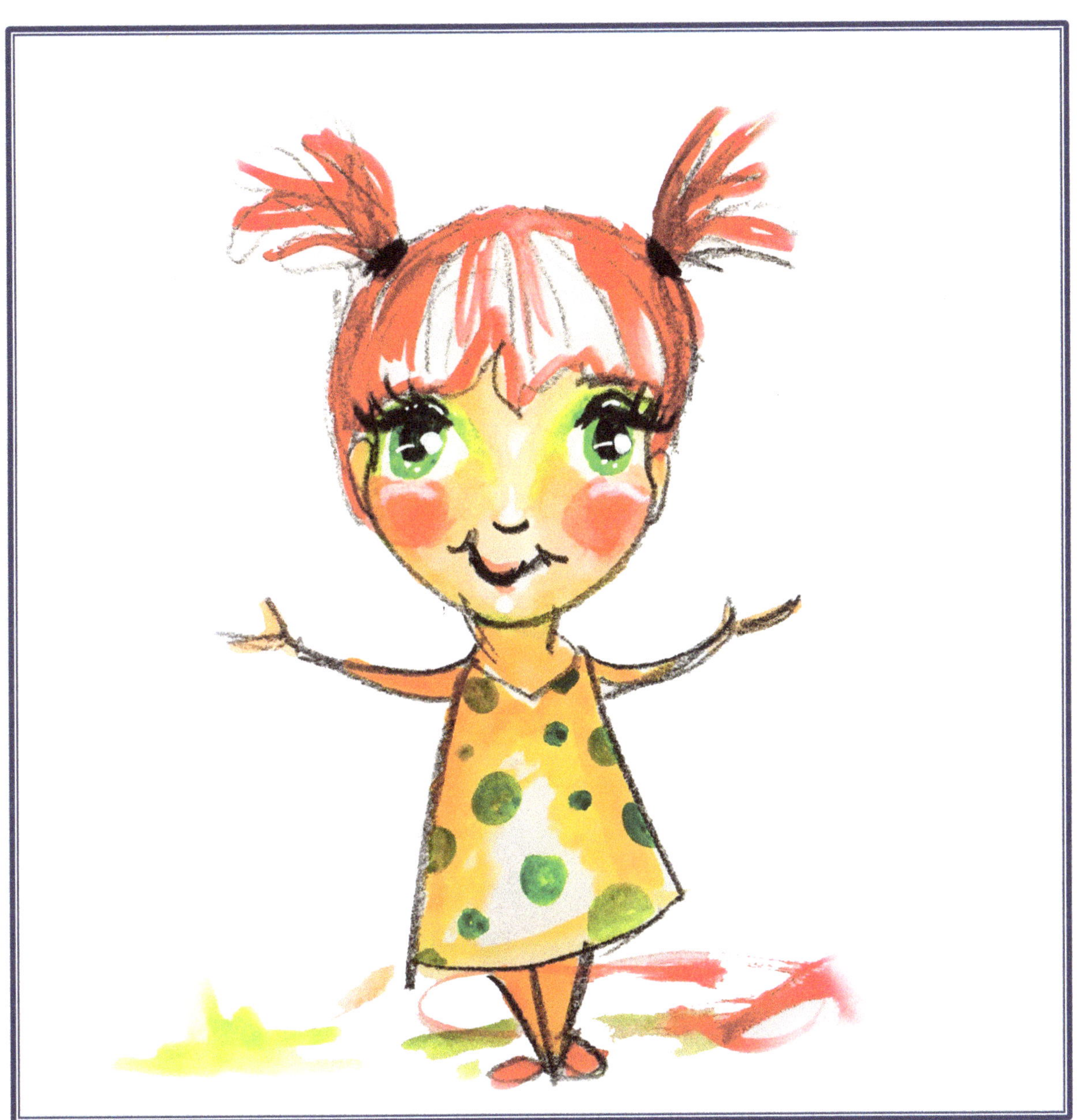

"The greater part of our happiness or misery
depends on our dispositions, and not on our
circumstances. We carry the seeds of the one
or the other about with us in our minds
wherever we go."

Martha Washington

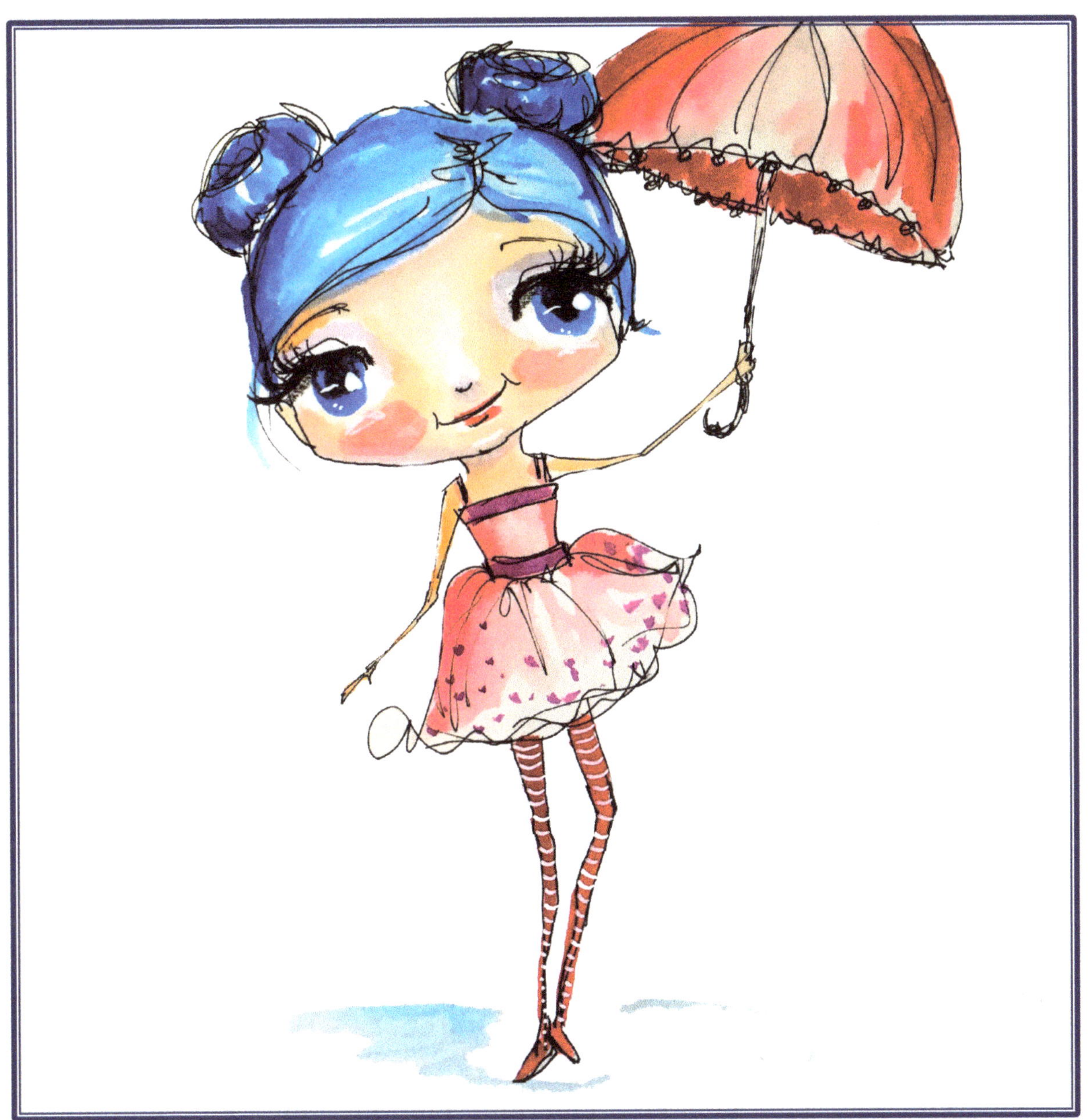

There is an old legend that within each of us there are
two wolves. One wolf is the fear, anger, jealousy and
misery. The other is joy, happiness, love and hope.

Which of these wolves would win in a fight?

The one you feed.

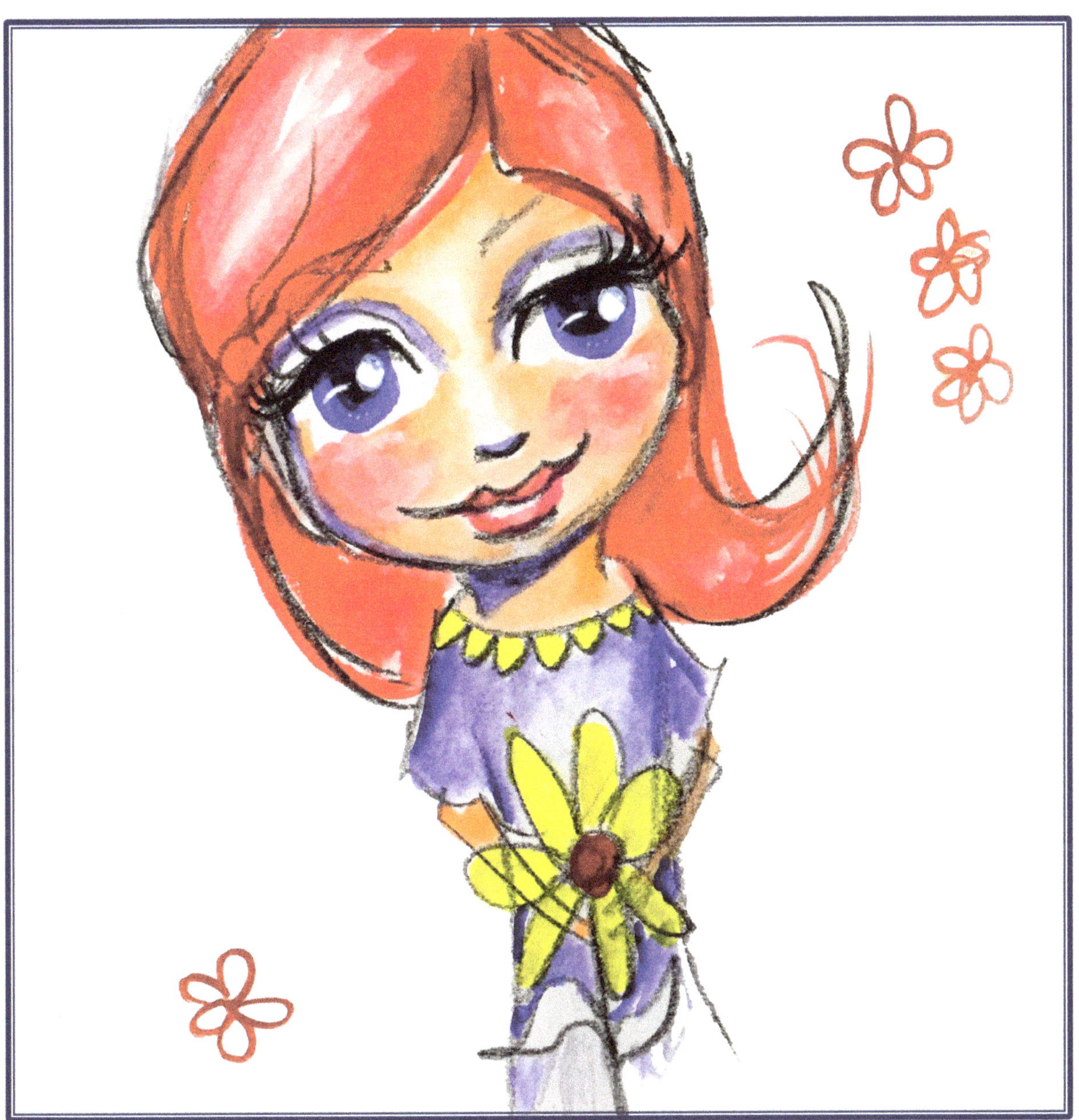

"Remember to light the candle of joy daily and all the gloom will disappear from your life."

Djwhal Khul

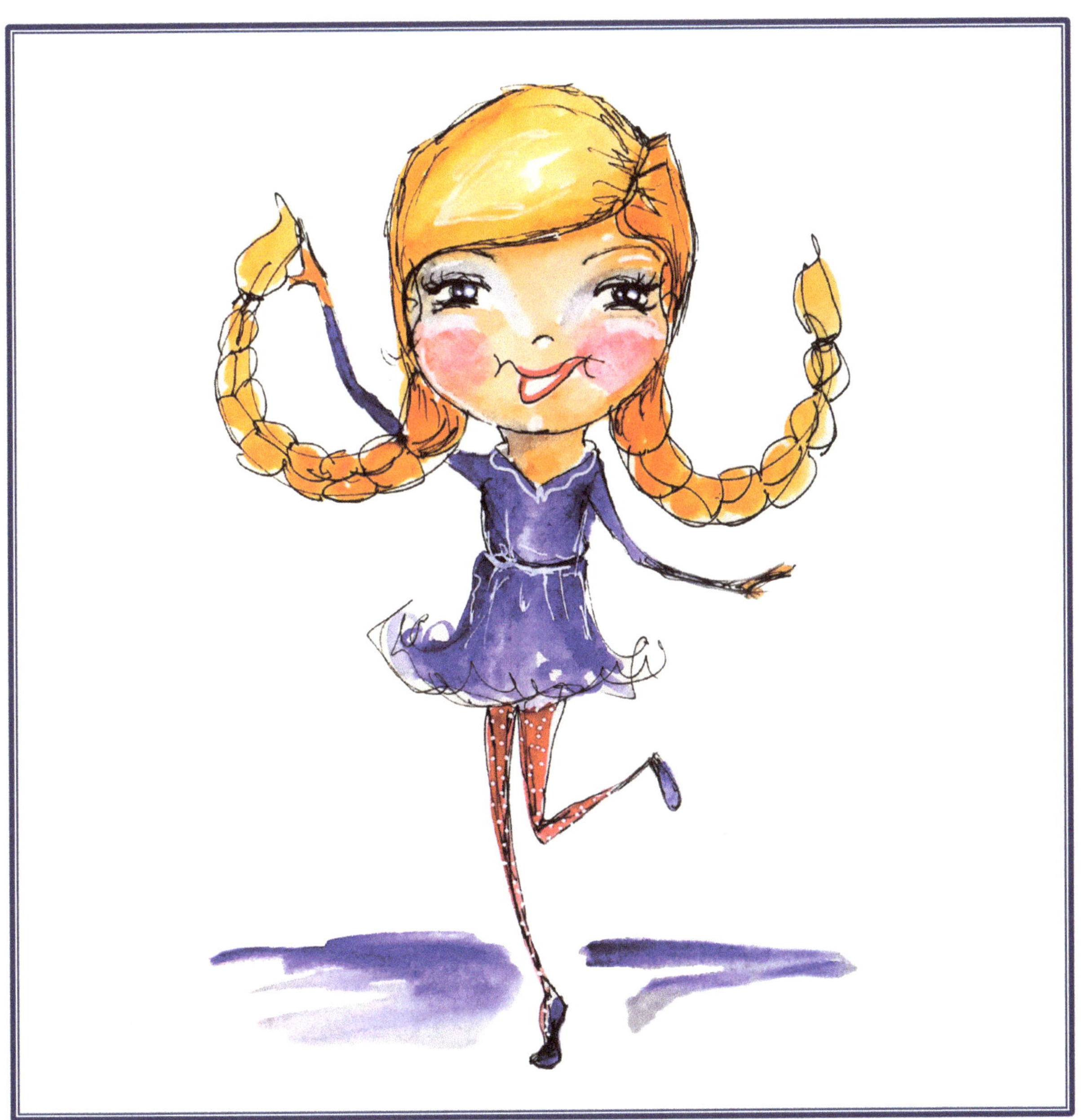

It is not the events and circumstances of our lives that make us happy or sad. These are simply facts - an occurrence or a non occurrence. It is the stories we tell ourselves about these events and circumstances that dictate our emotional response.

Fortunately, the one thing over which we have complete control is these stories.

Choose wisely. Choose joy.

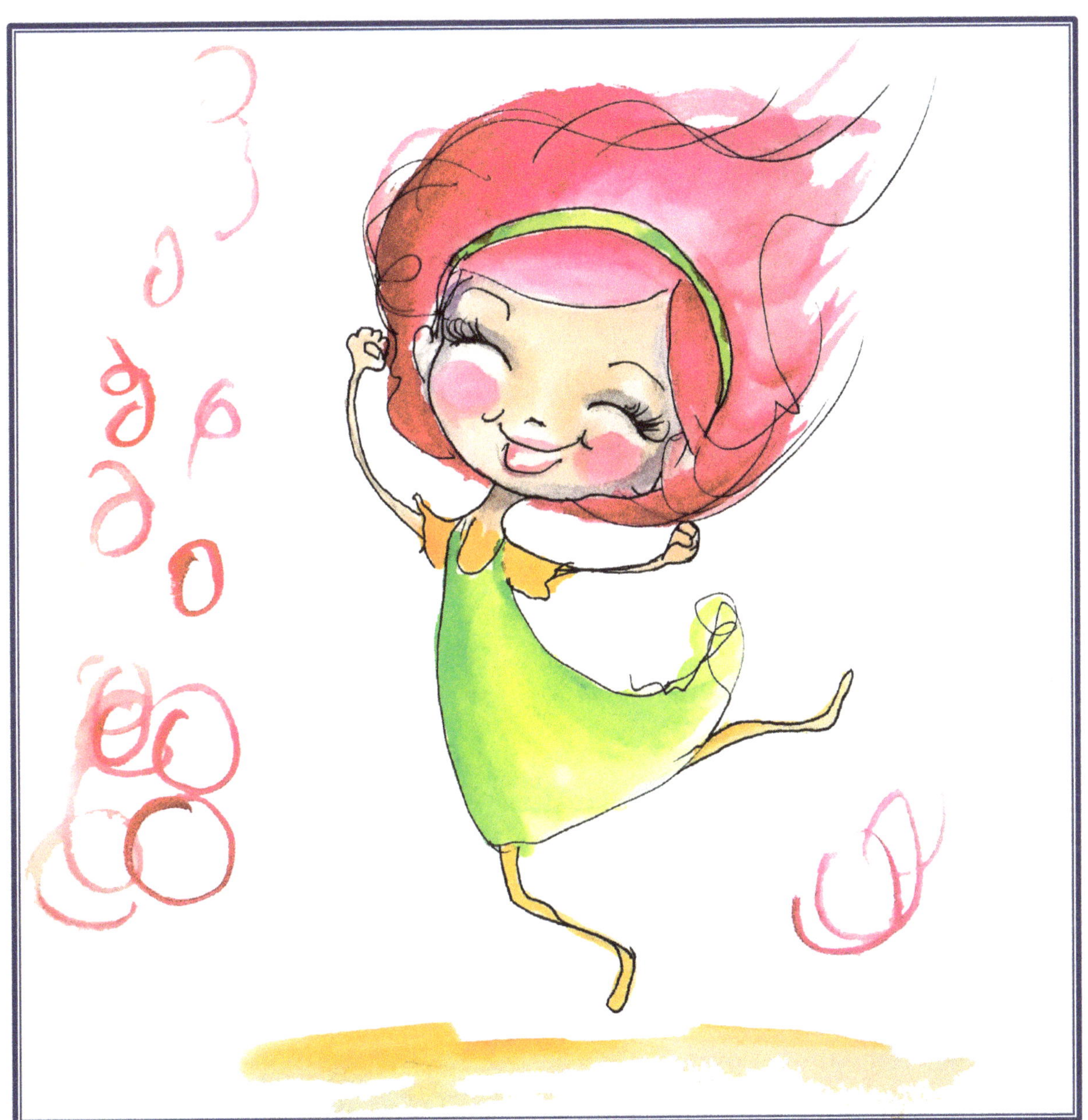

"Everything can be taken away from a man but one thing: the last of the human freedoms - to choose one's attitude in any given set of circumstances, to choose one's own way."

Viktor E. Frankl

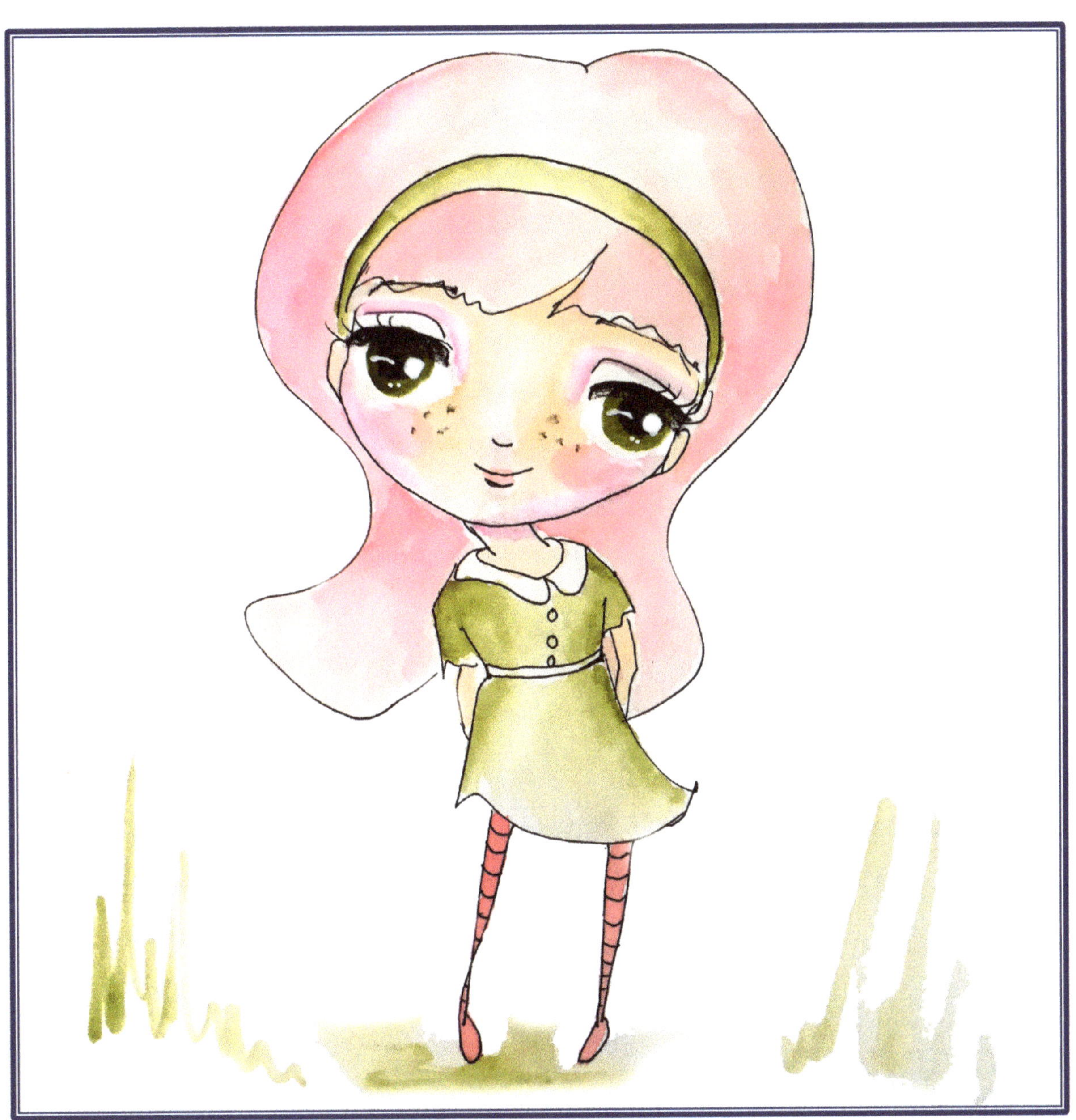

"Happiness does not depend on outward things, but on the way we see them."

Count Leo Tolstoy

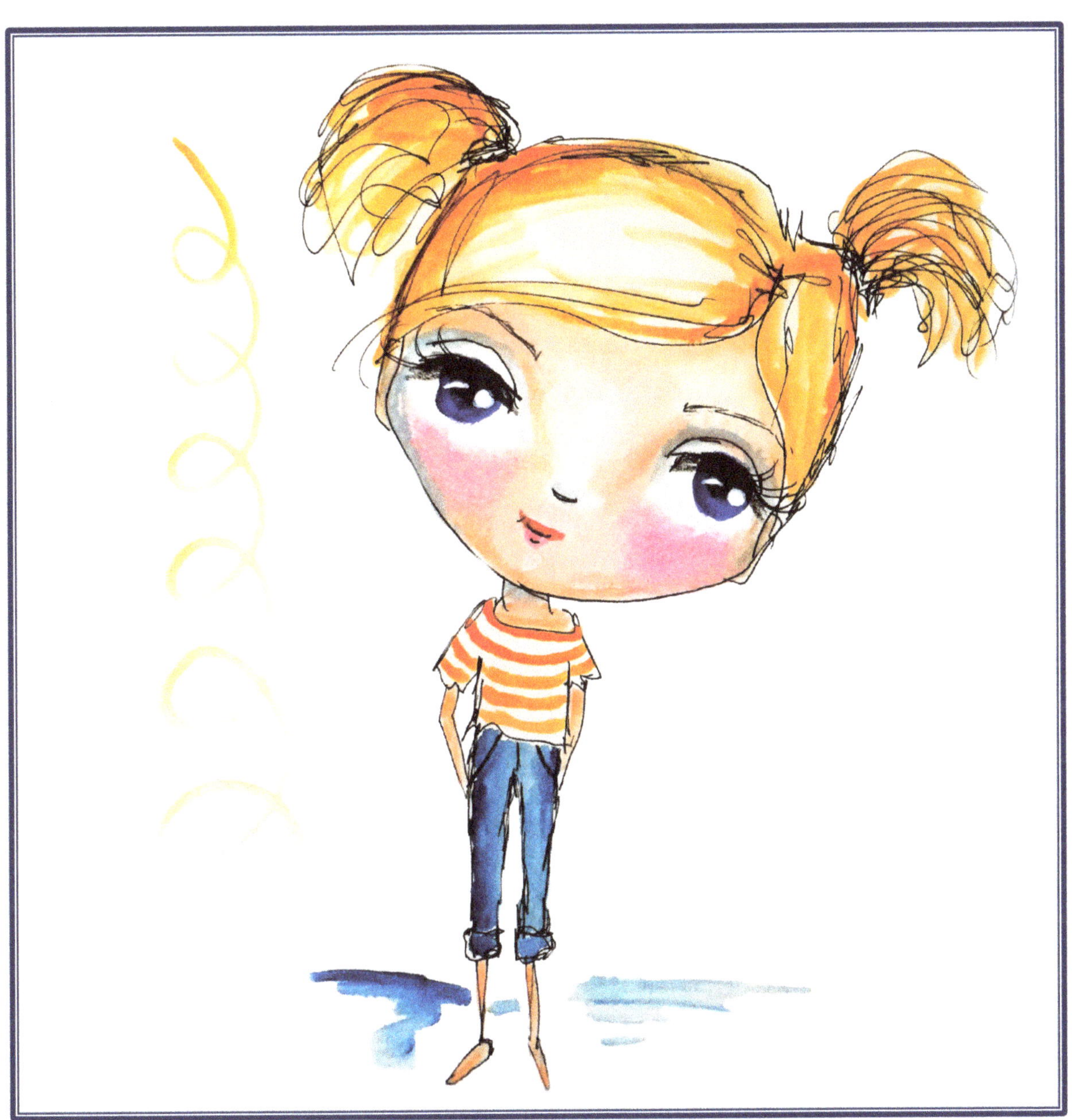

The negative experiences of our lives and the voices of doubt and fear loom large, demanding our attention. We are even biologically programmed to pay attention to them for our own safety.

If happiness is our goal, our task is to remember that the positive experiences and the tiny moments of joy are there - *at least* in equal measure. But they have quieter voices and make no demands. They need our awareness and our consistent effort to keep the balance.

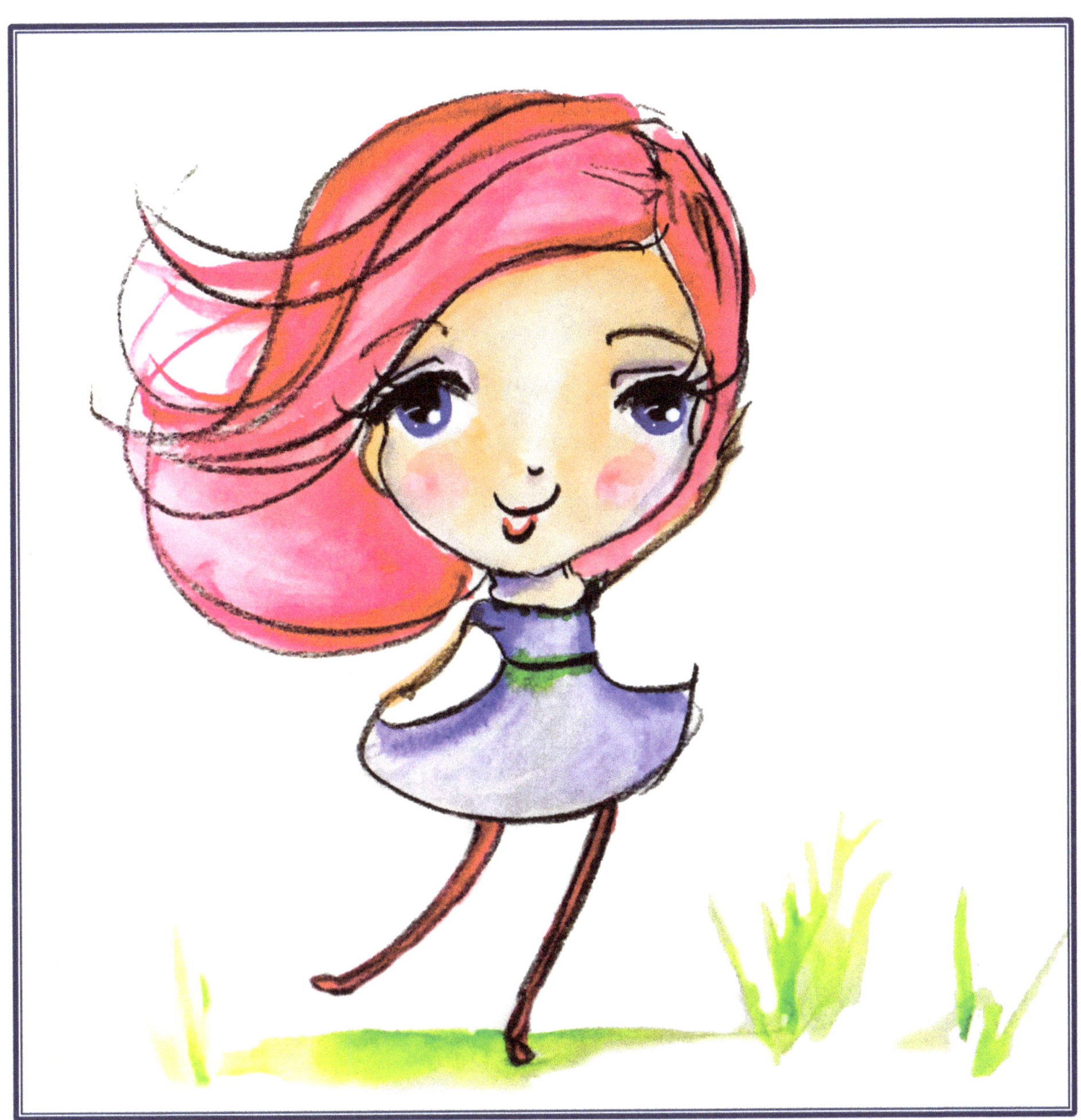

"Find a place inside where there's joy, and
the joy will burn out the pain."

Joseph Campbell

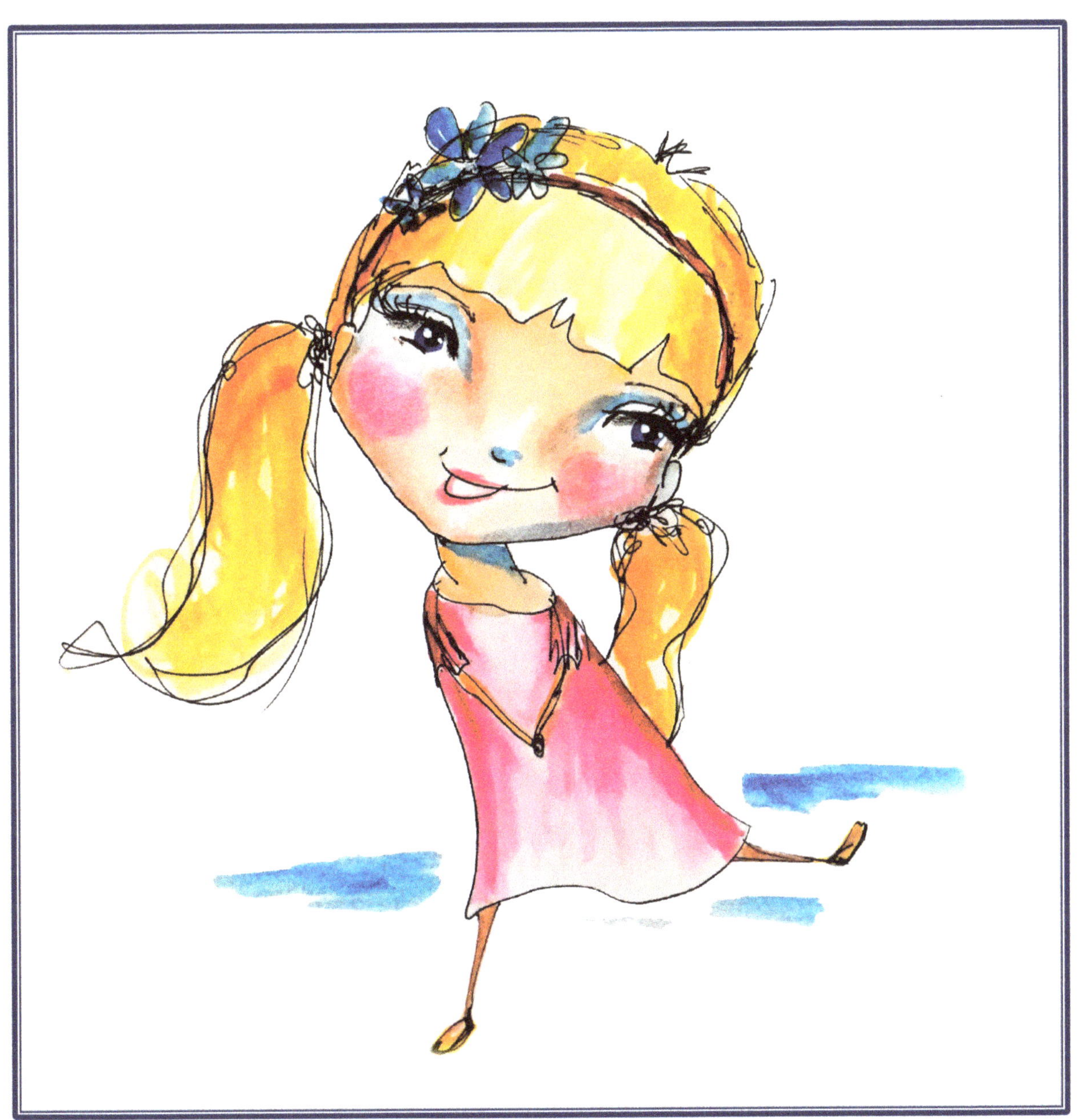

Reframing your outlook

We are the artists in our lives, observing the world landscape through the lens of our own perception. Our gaze takes in all that is before us, good or bad. Like a photographer, we get to choose our focal point.

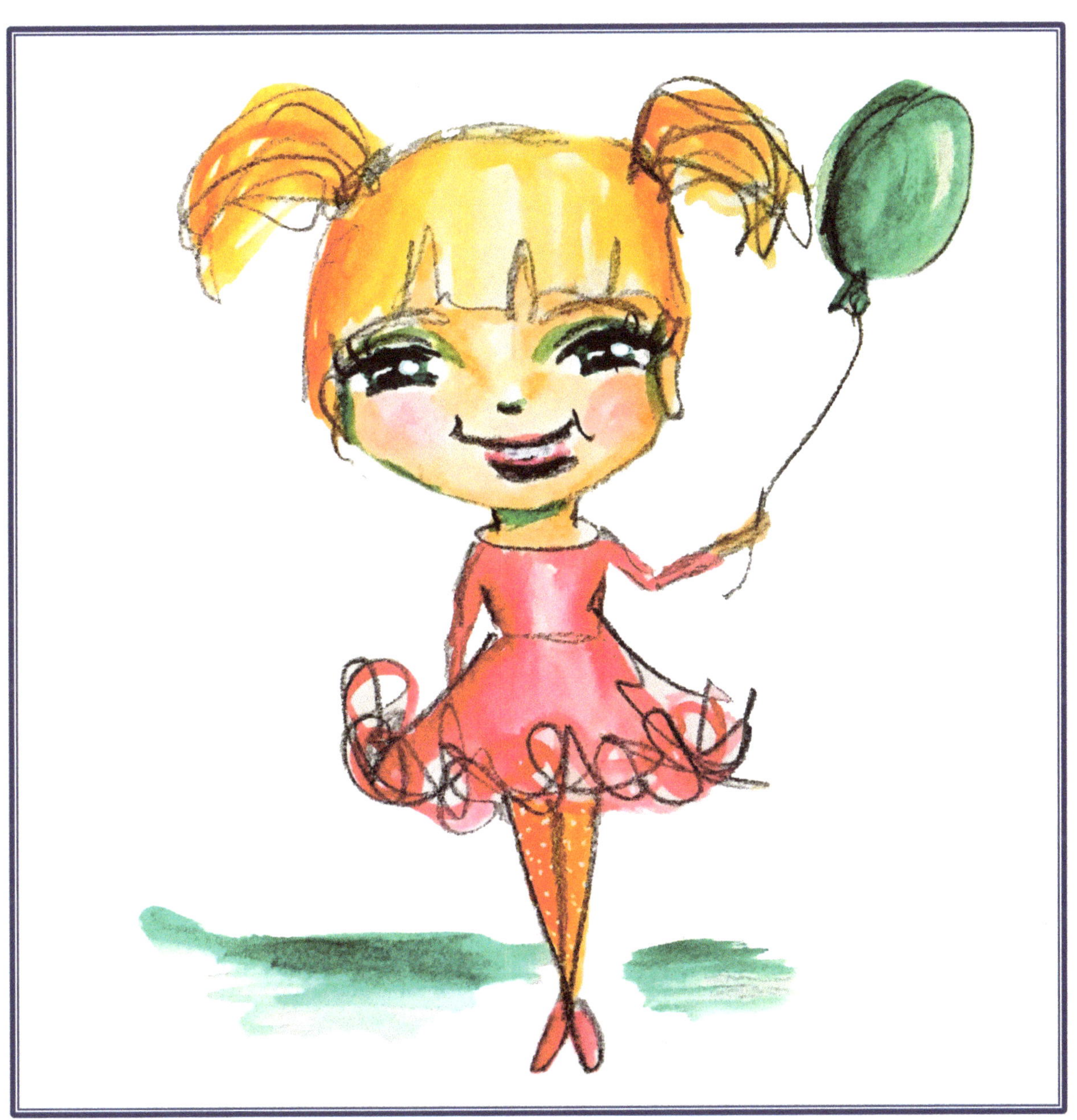

"The joy we feel has little to do with the circumstances of our lives and everything to do with the focus of our lives."

Russel M Nelson

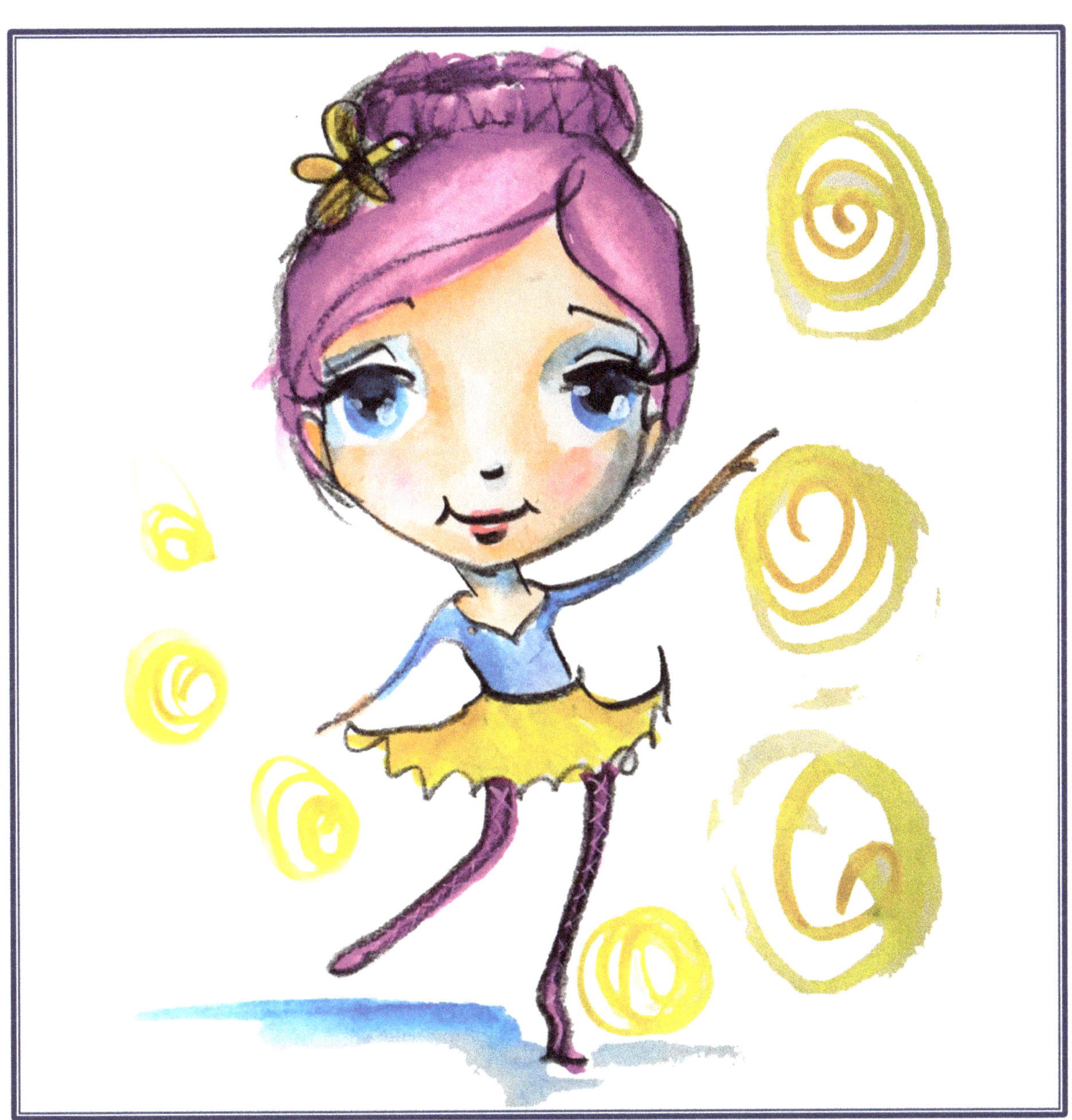

What we choose to focus on determines the prevailing feeling of the whole image. It is not that there is nothing unhappy or difficult in the world. While these things are still there we can choose to allow them to blur into the background while we channel our attention towards the things that bring us joy.

Let these things take centre stage. Relish their fine details. Let them be vibrant in glorious technicolour.

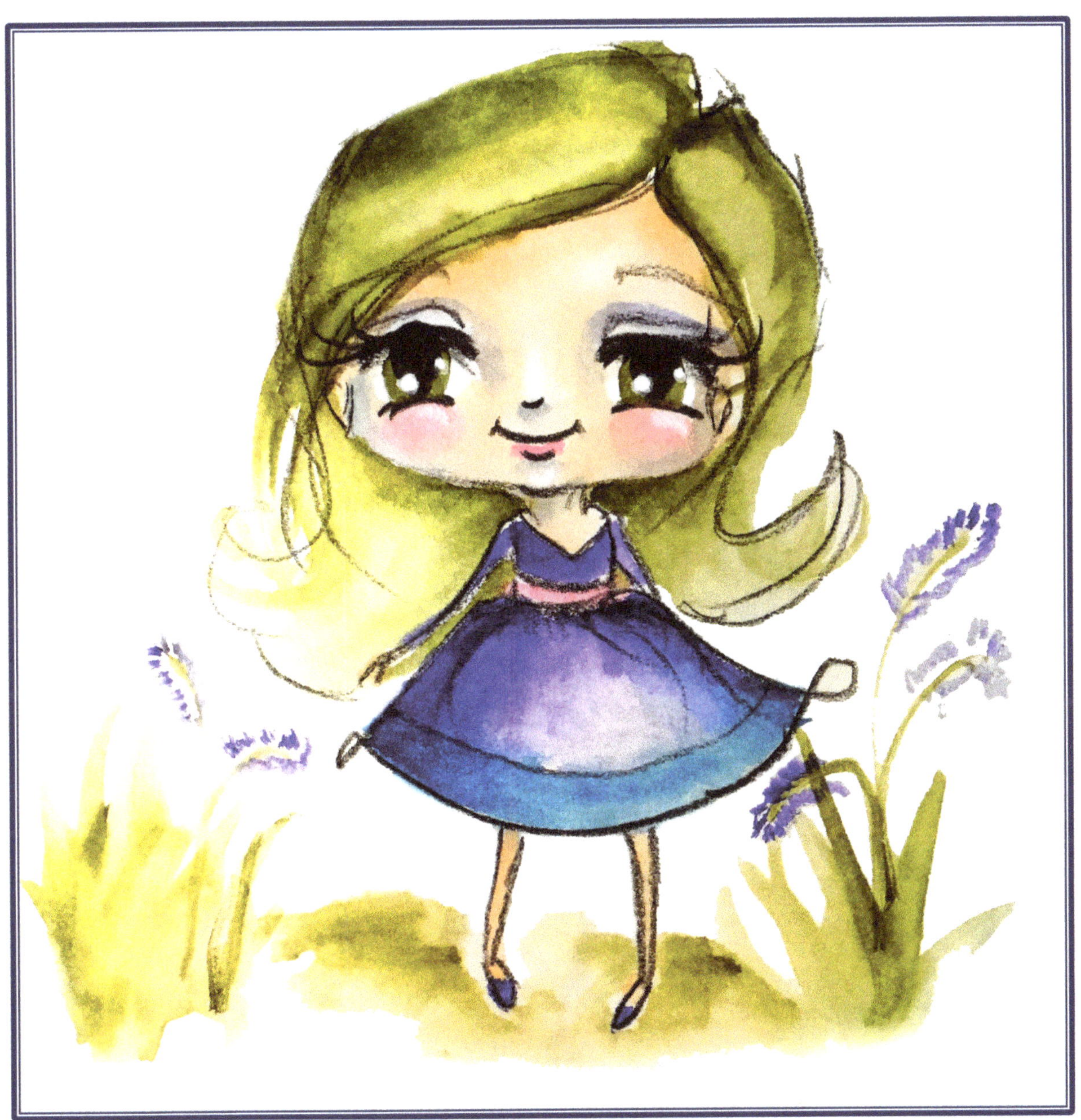

"To get up each morning with the resolve to be happy is to set our own conditions to the events of each day. To do this is to condition circumstances instead of being conditioned by them."

Ralph Waldo Emerson

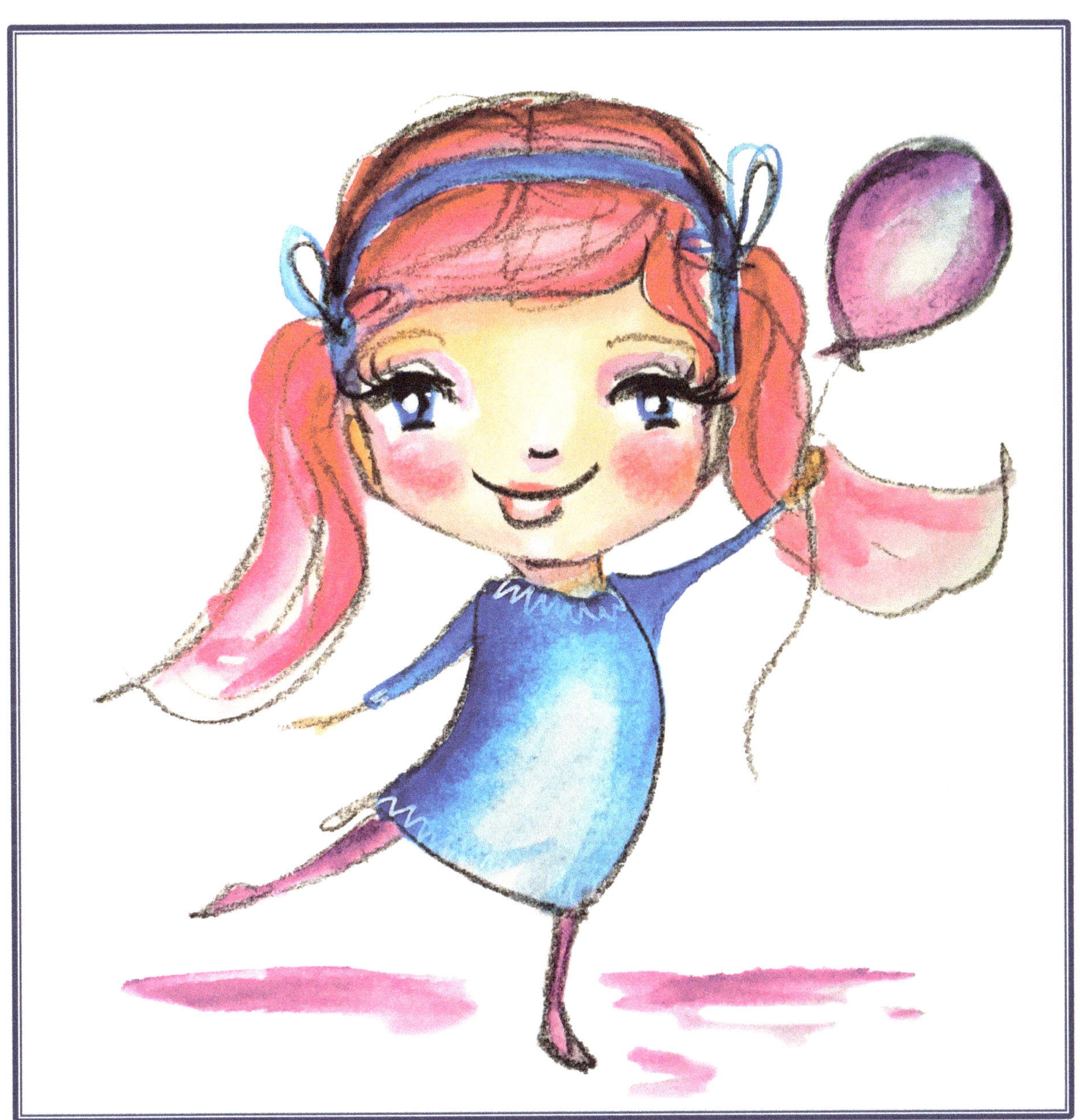

"Joy does not simply happen to us. We have
to choose joy and keep choosing it every
day."

Henri Nouwen

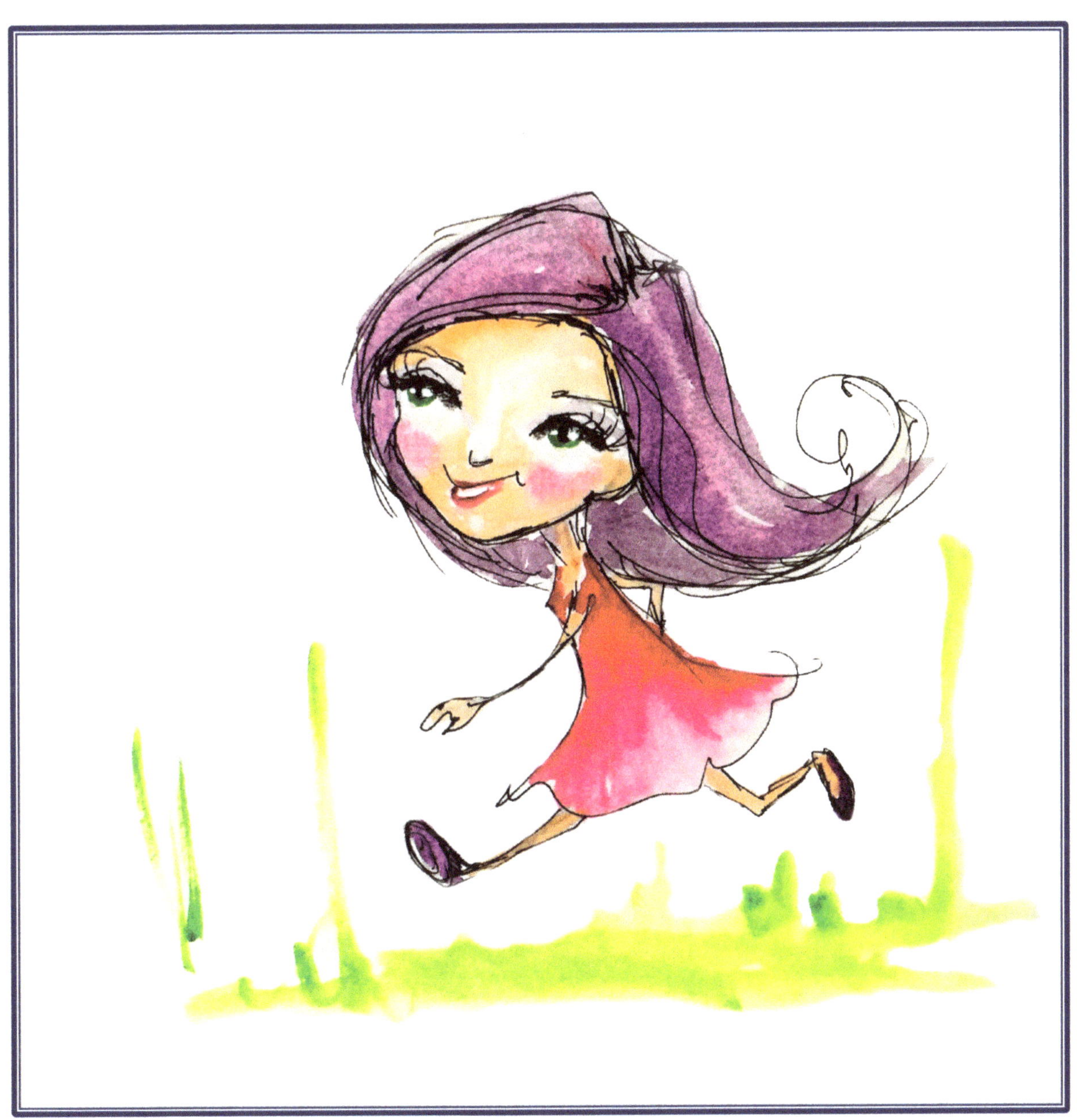

Joy as a guide

We travel through the world looking for signs. Some indication that we are on the right path, making the right choices. Joy is our most reliable sign - the beacon illuminating our true course.

We need not look for it in the world around us. We carry it within. Learn its full spectrum from wild jubilation to quiet contentment.

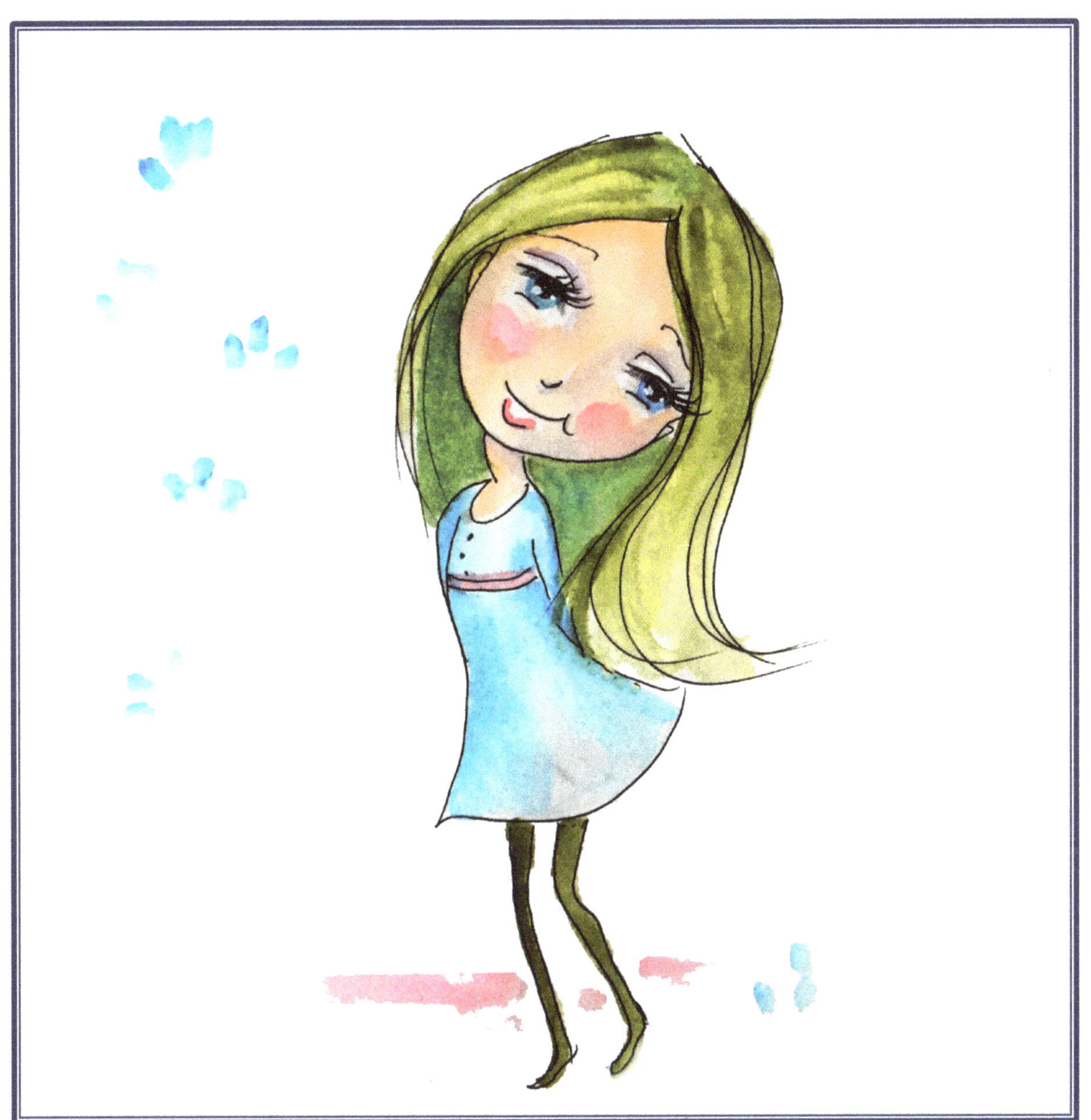

"When we are centred in joy, we attain our wisdom."

Marianne Williamson

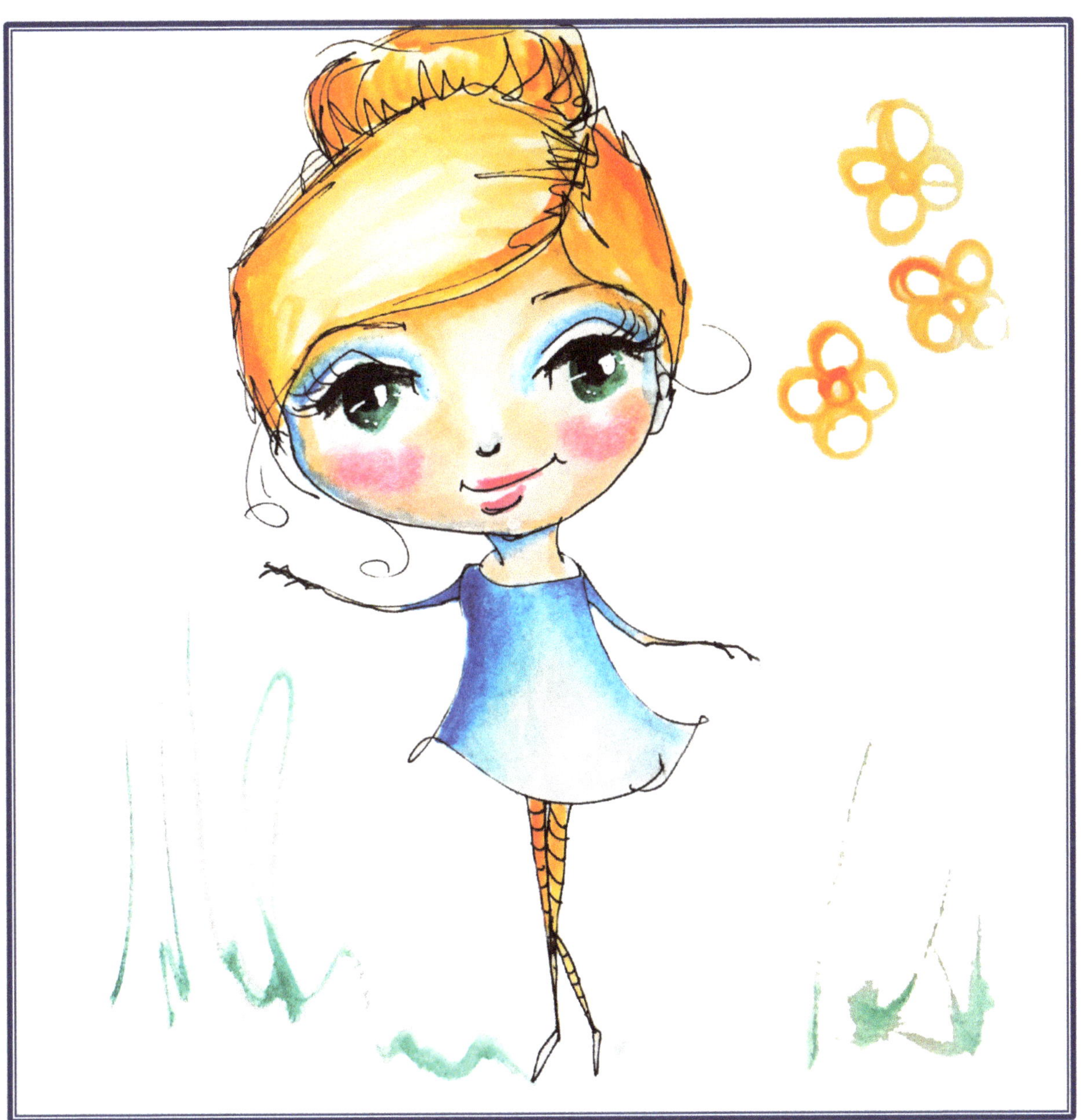

When you are faced with a decision, however big or small, your joy can be your compass and your guide. It is the voice of your inner wisdom.

Trust that it will illuminate the choice that is in the highest and best interests of everyone concerned.

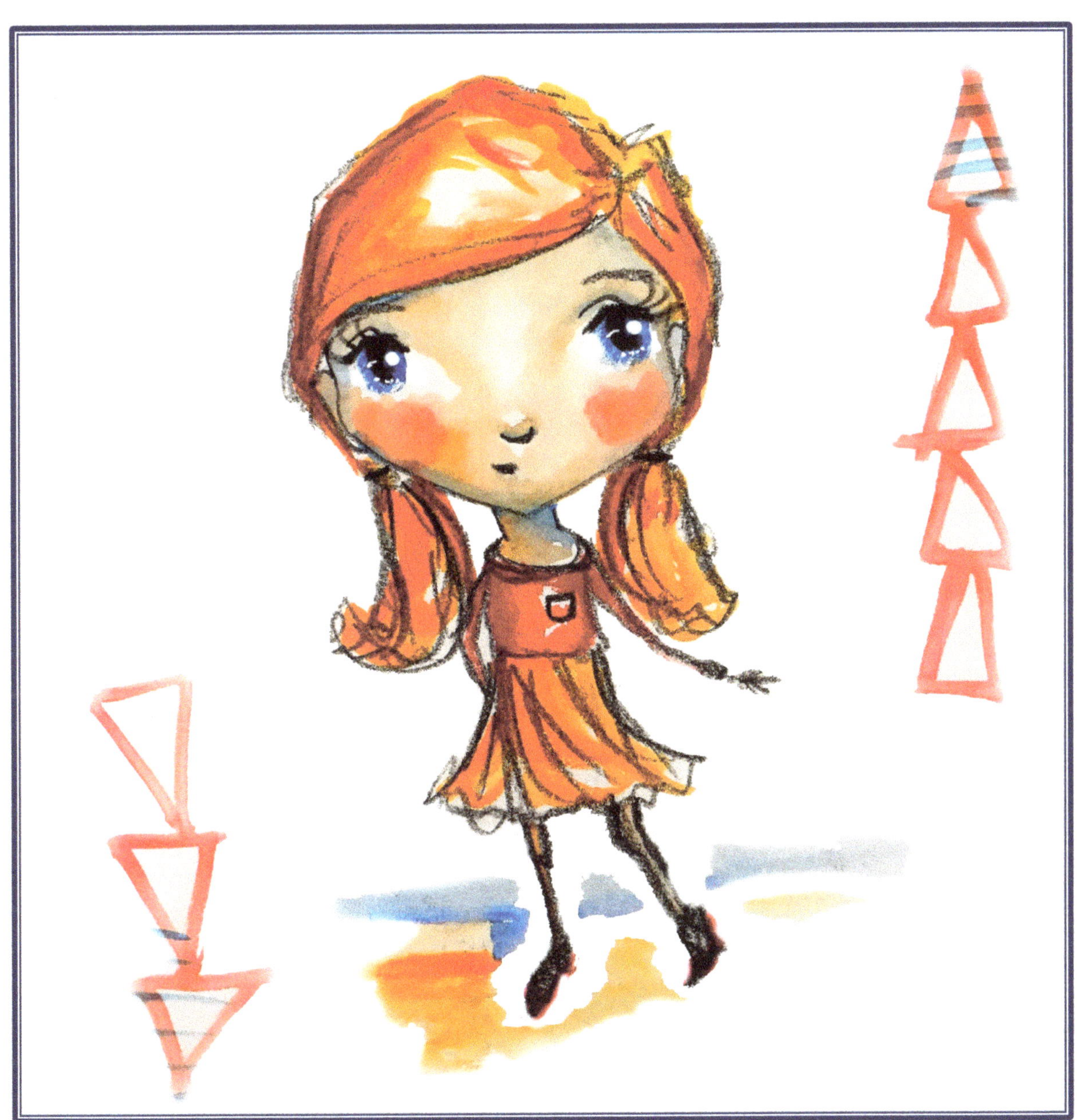

"Joy is our goal, our destiny. We cannot
know who we are except in Joy. Not knowing
Joy, we do not know ourselves."

Marianne Williamson

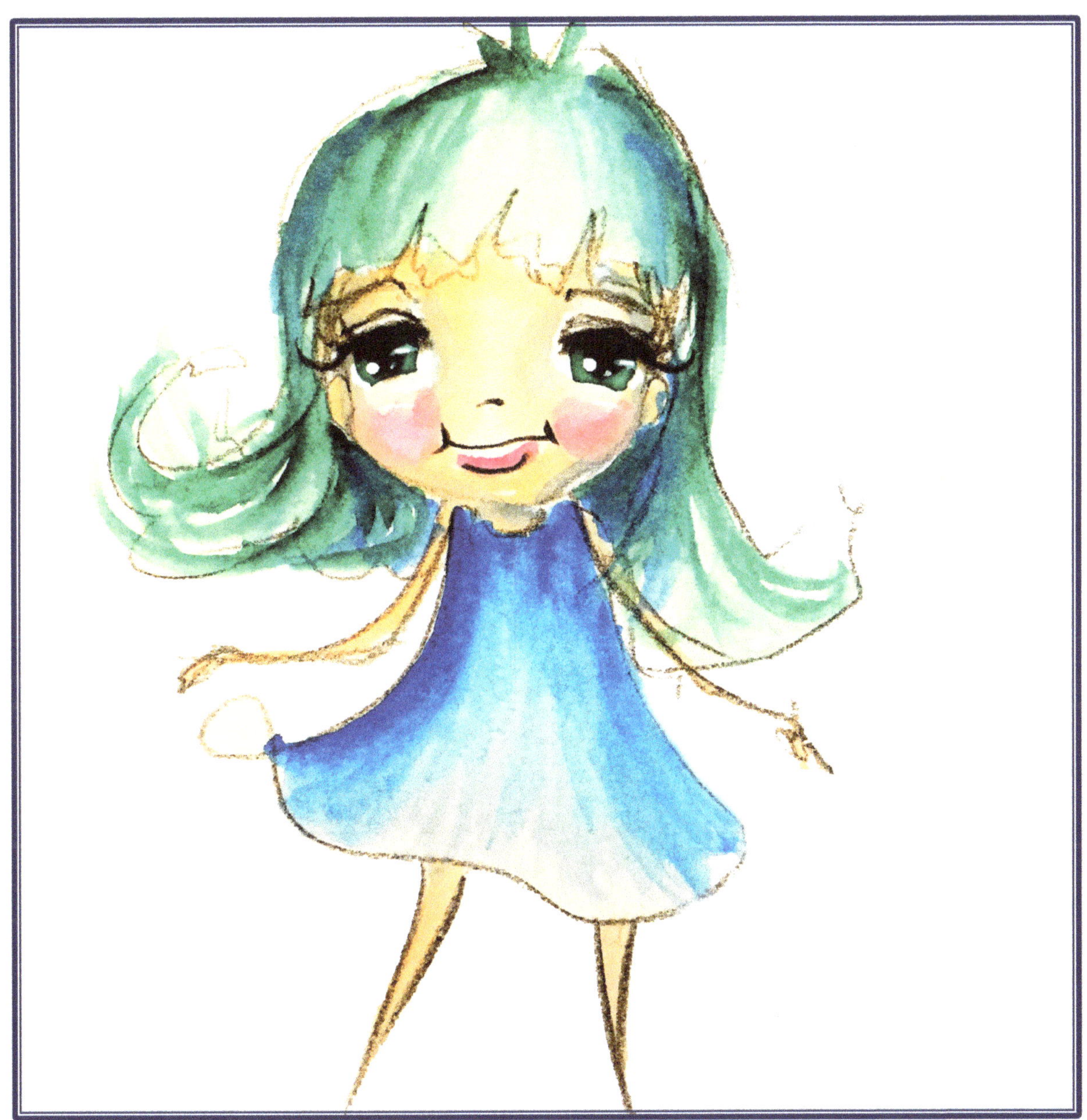

What joy is

Choosing joy is a matter of rediscovering the things that light up your life. These are often not big things. They are the simple pleasures that allow us to find the beauty in the everyday.

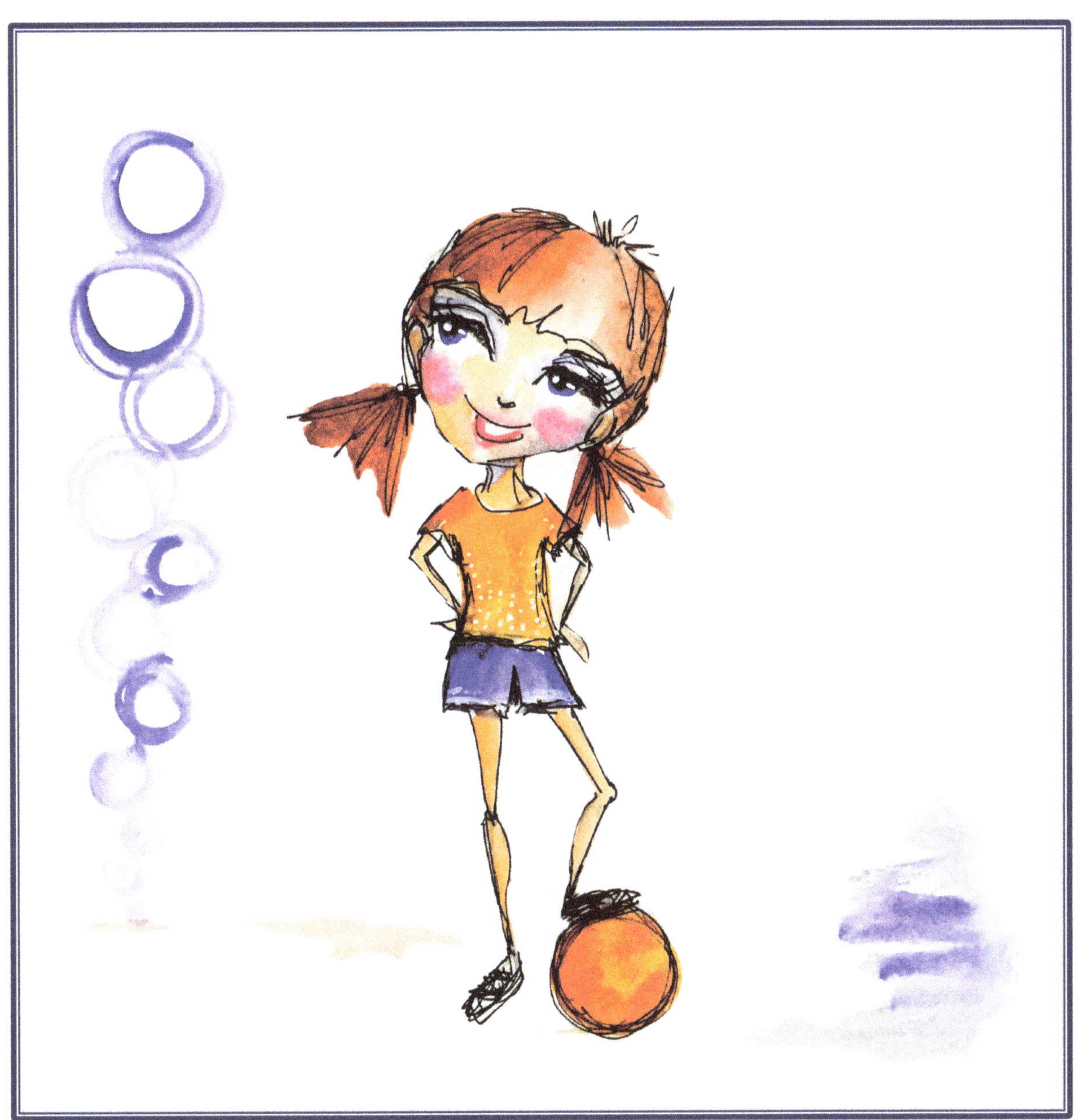

"Joy comes to us in ordinary moments. We
risk missing out when we get too busy
chasing down the extraordinary."

Brene Brown

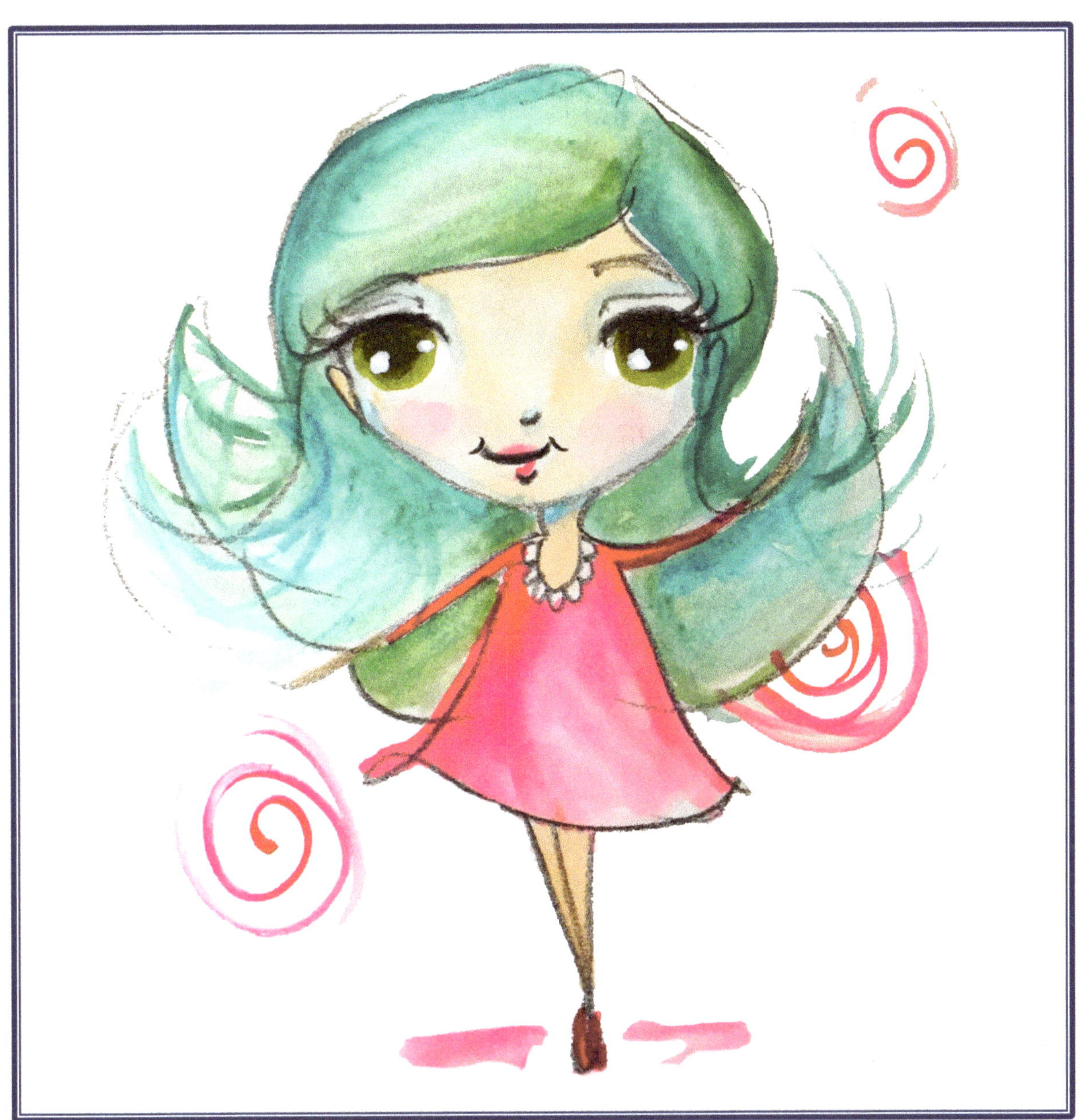

"True joy is that which gives us more energy
and makes us feel more alive."

Robert Puryear

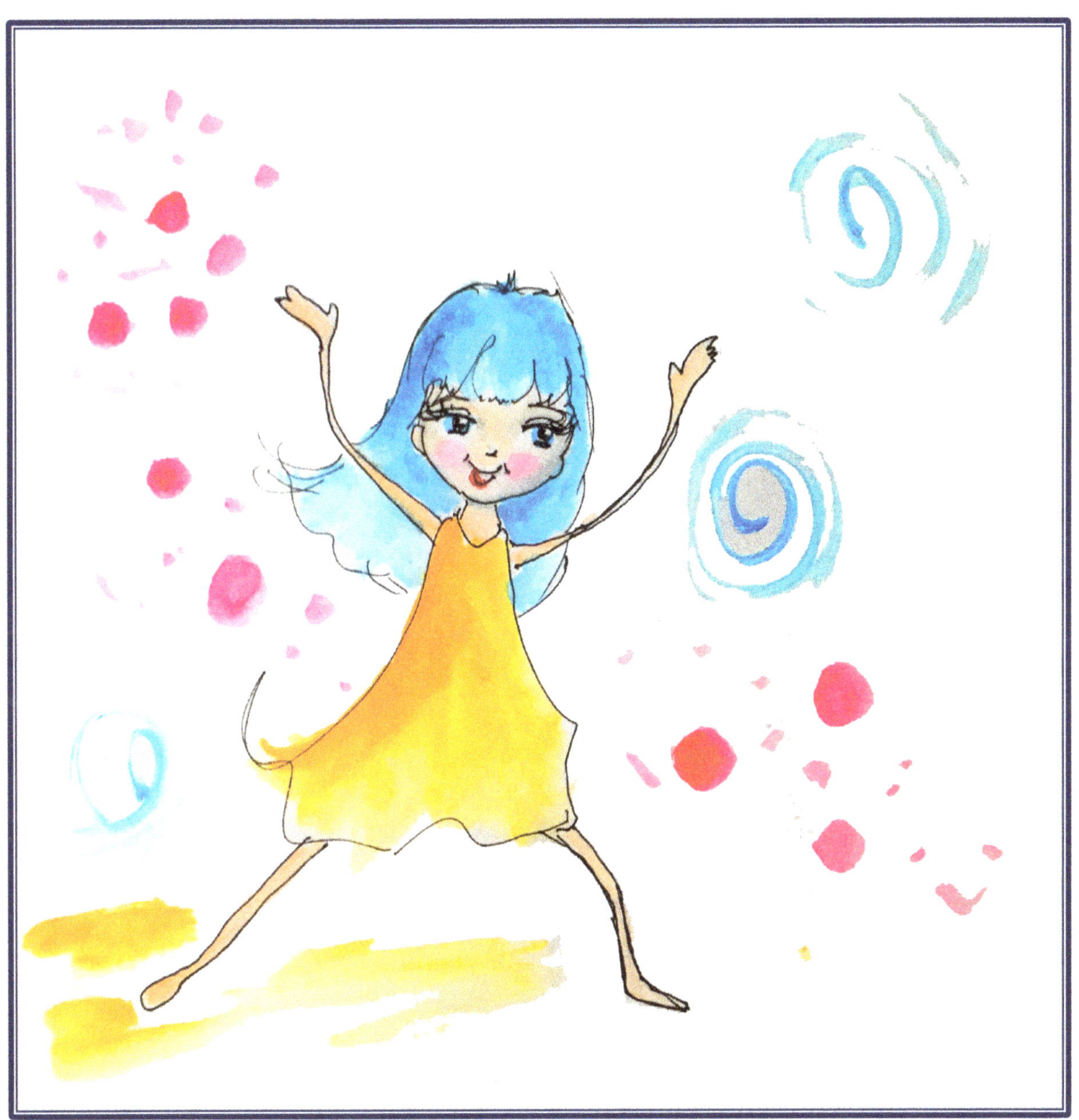

"Sometimes your joy is the source of your smile, but sometimes your smile can be the source of your joy."

Thich Nhat Hanh

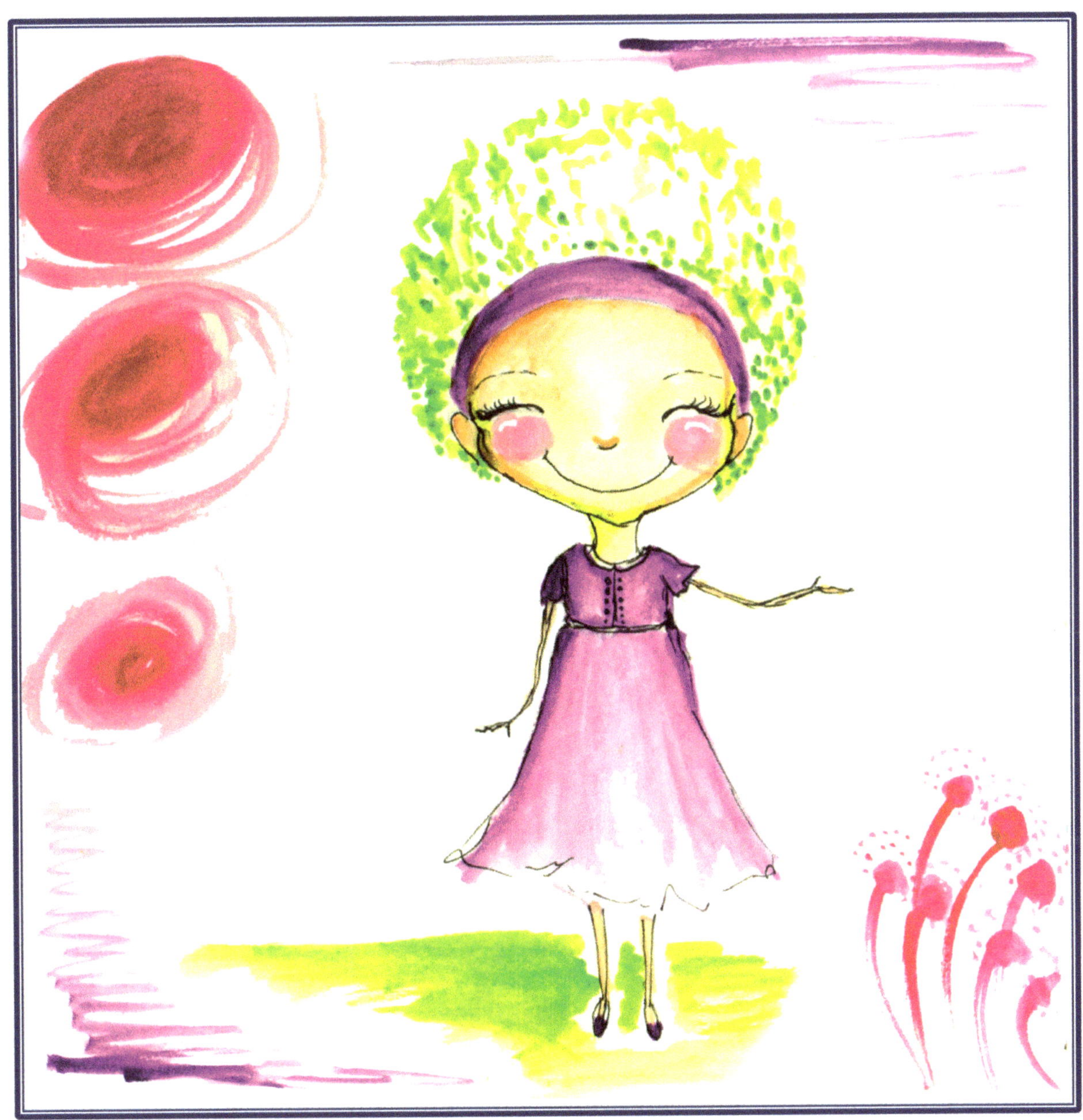

It is your responsibility to follow your joy. The things that you enjoy and that you are best at are what lights your soul.

And what the world needs is souls that are alight.

Your joy is contagious.

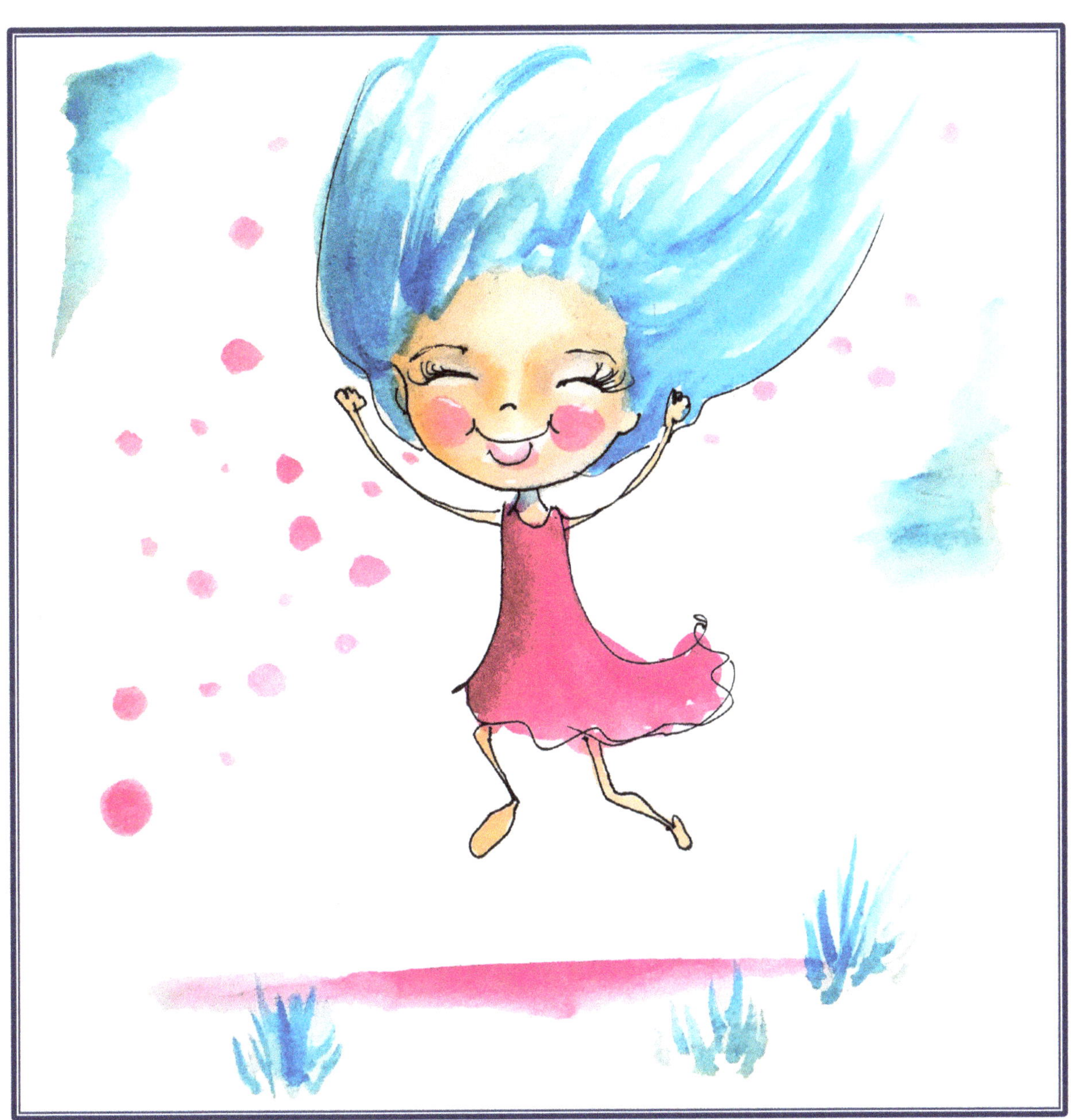

"Find out where joy resides, and give it a
voice far beyond singing. For to miss the joy
is to miss all."

Robert Louis Stevenson

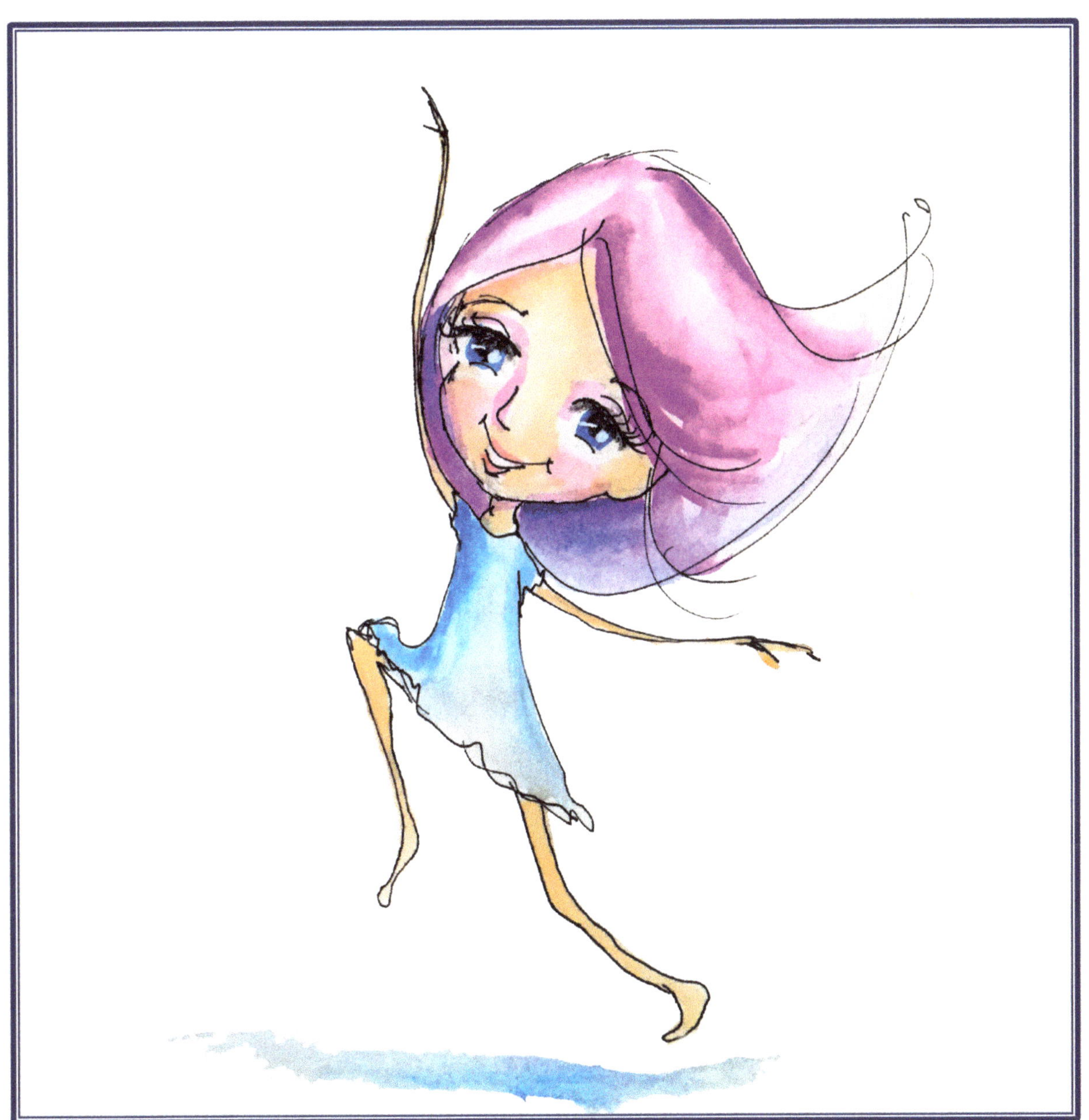

Your energy serves its highest purpose when you do what brings you joy. This is where you serve the world in the best way that you can.

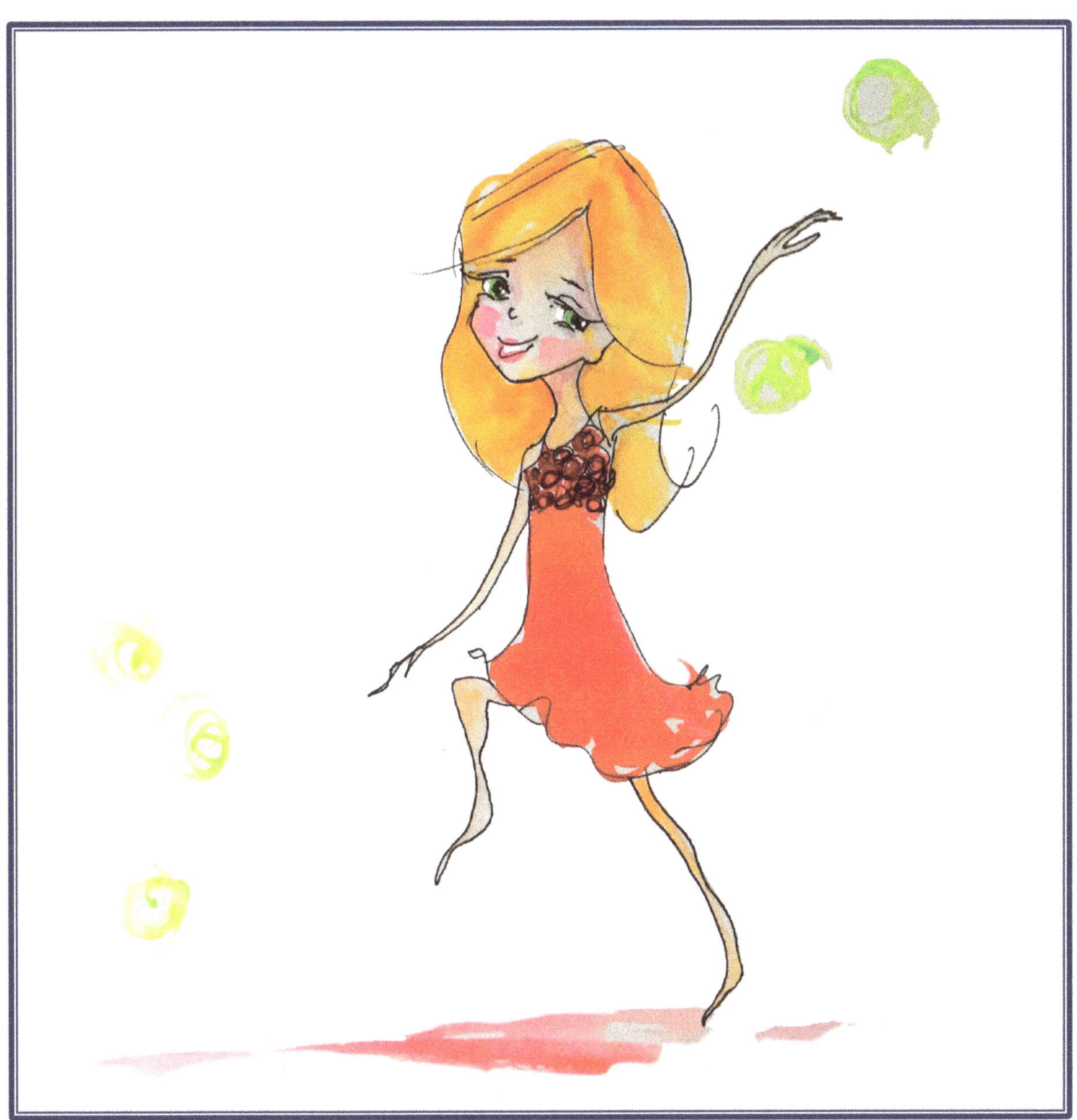

"May all beings learn how to nourish themselves with joy each day."

Thich Nhat Hanh

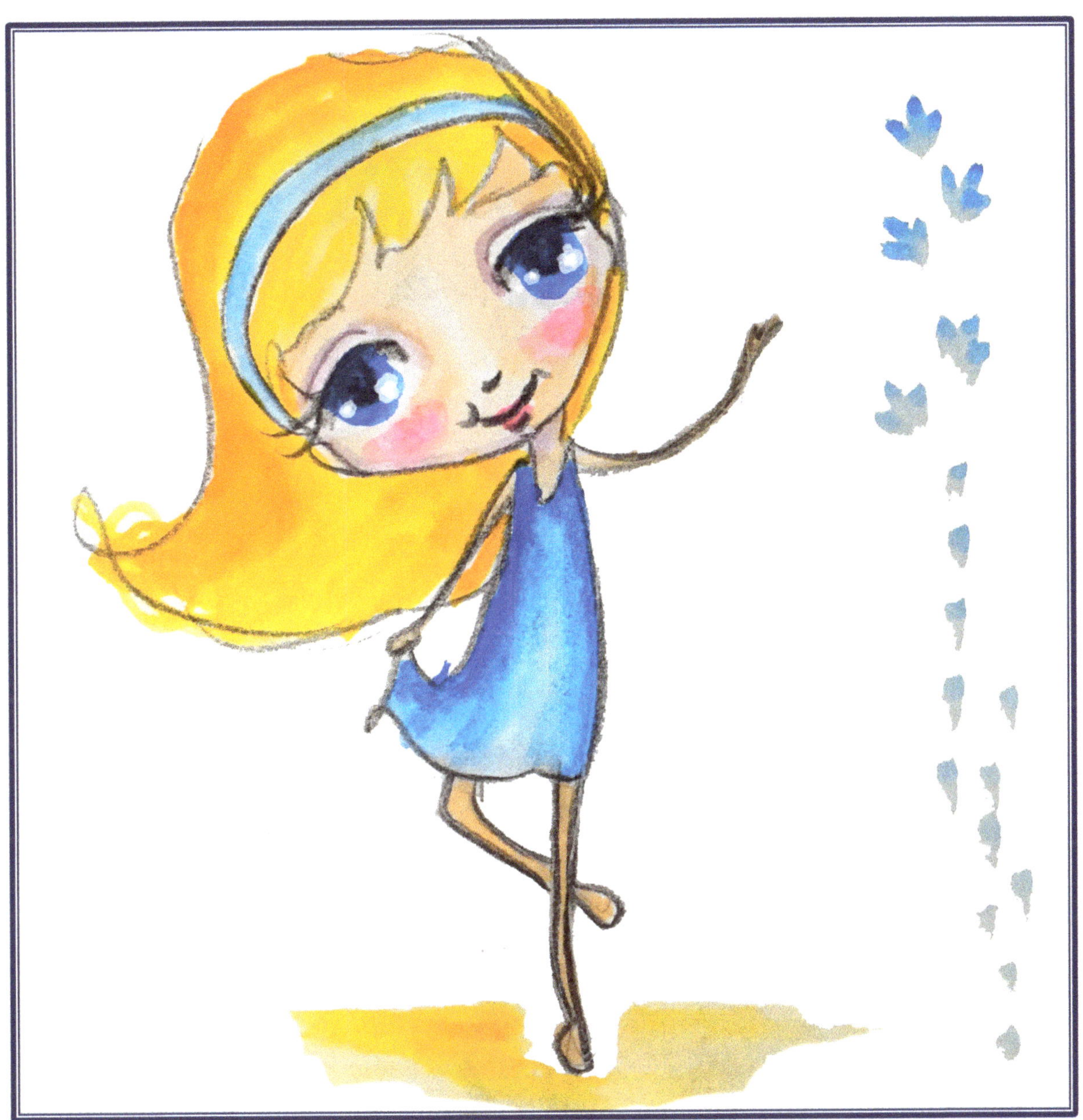

Those that are happy and empowered encourage those around them to do the same.

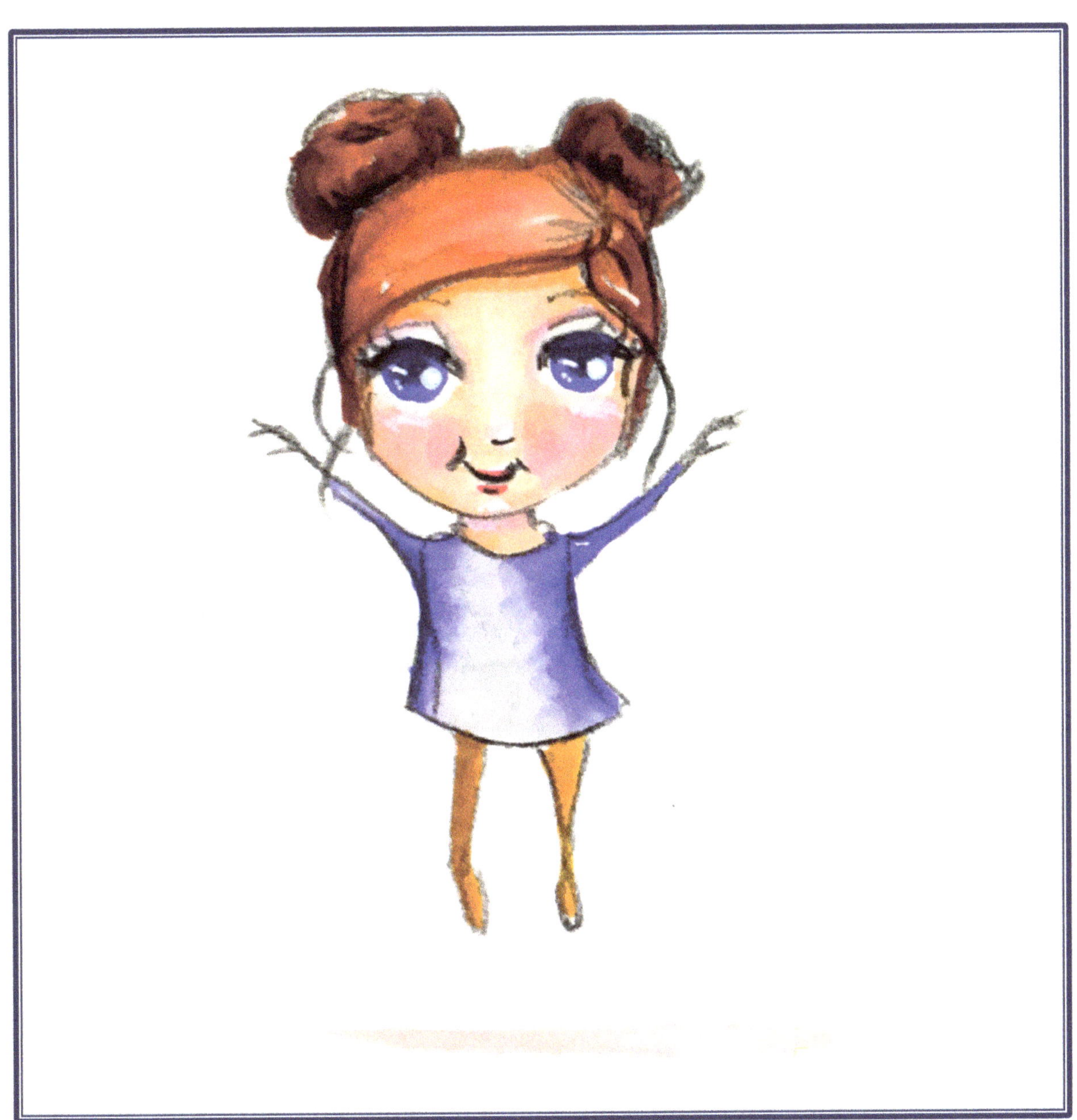

"There are souls in this world which have the gift of finding joy everywhere and of leaving it behind when they go."

Frederick Wm. Faber

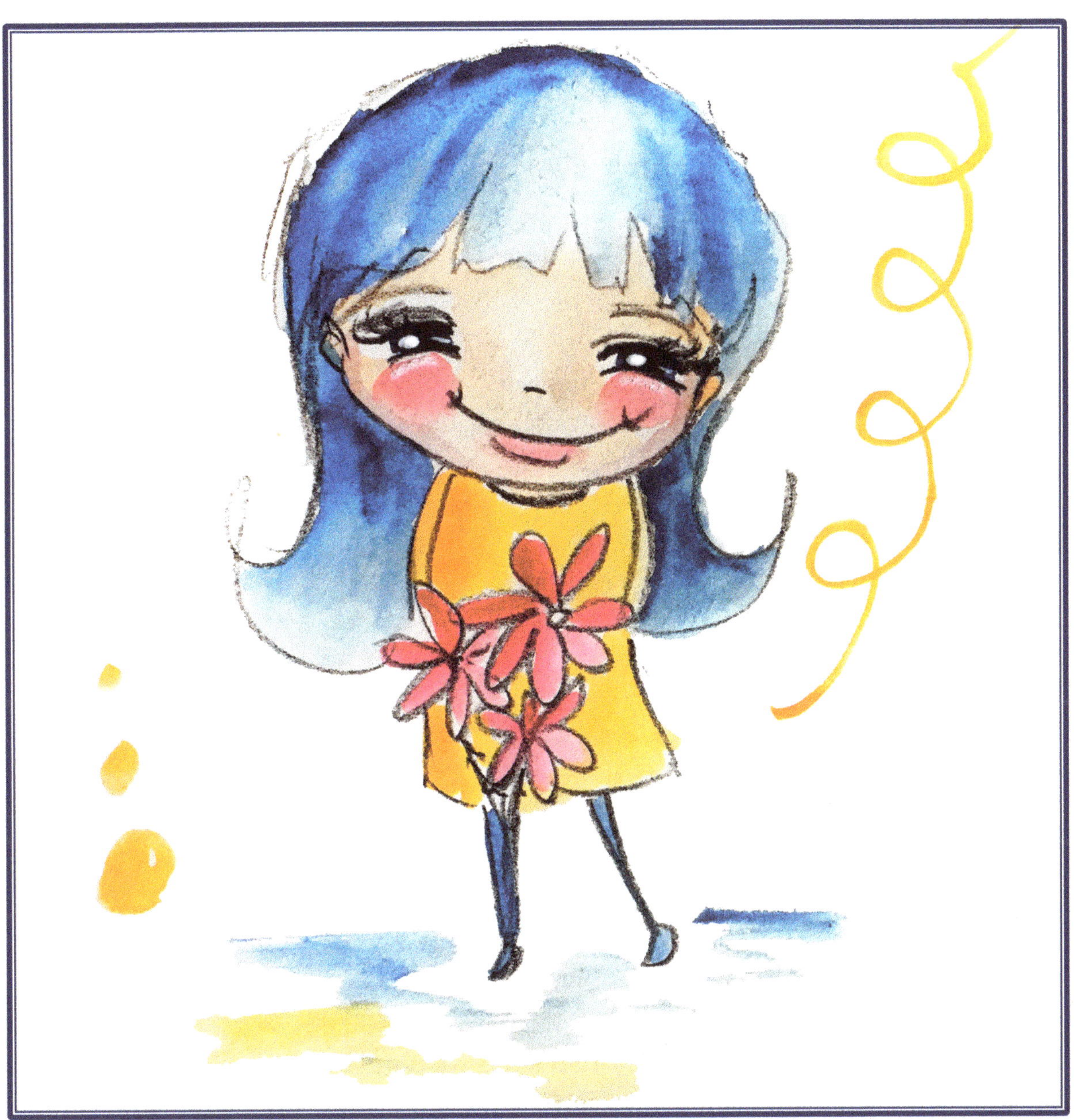

Measure your success by the amount of joy you can experience.

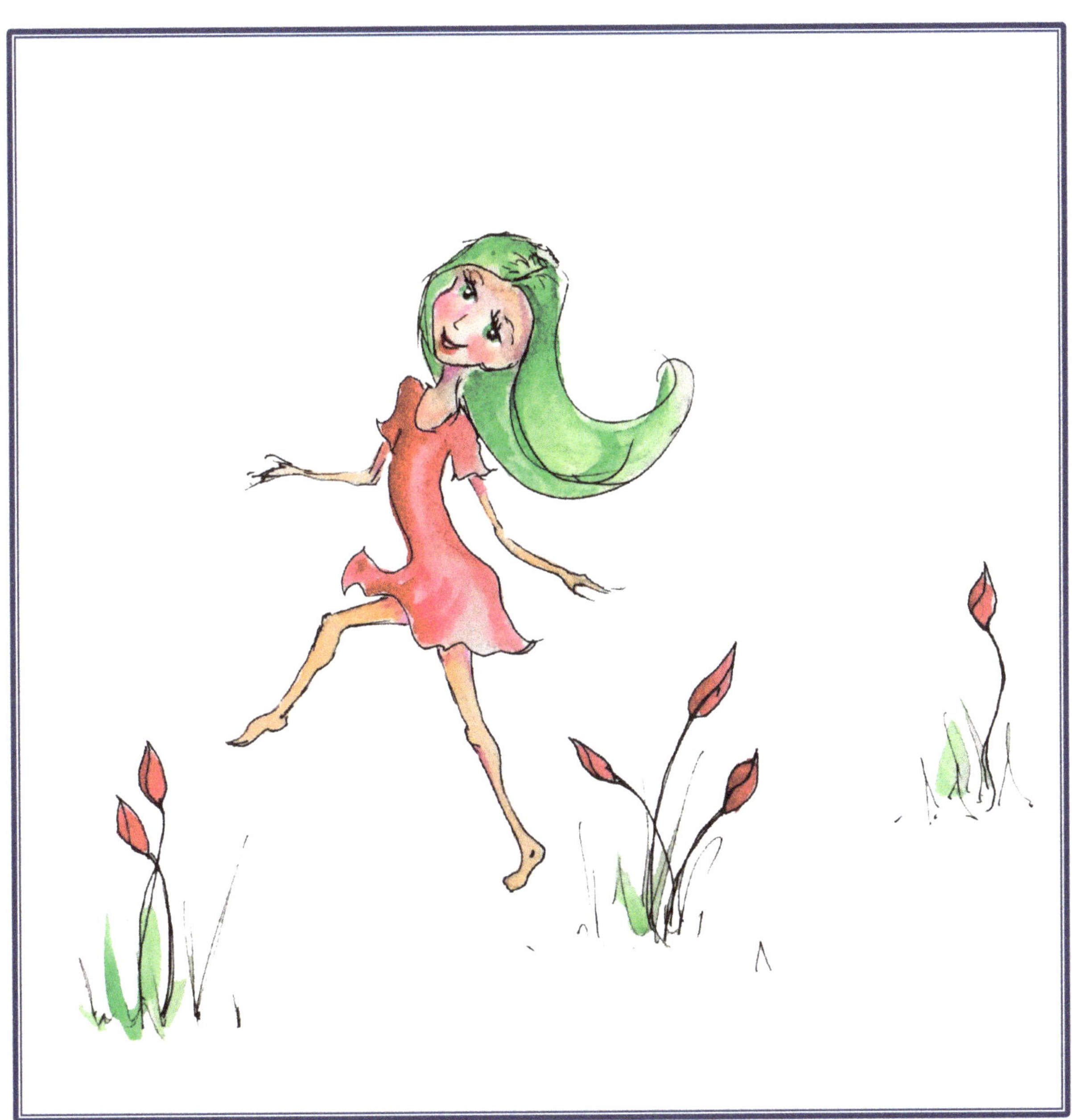

Joy is the spring in your step, the sunshine in your smile. It is the tickle of feathers within your ribcage, the dance of moonbeams up your spine. It is the bubbles of elation that rise and spill from your soul. It is the energy that makes your movements effortless.

It is the essence of you.

Choose Joy.

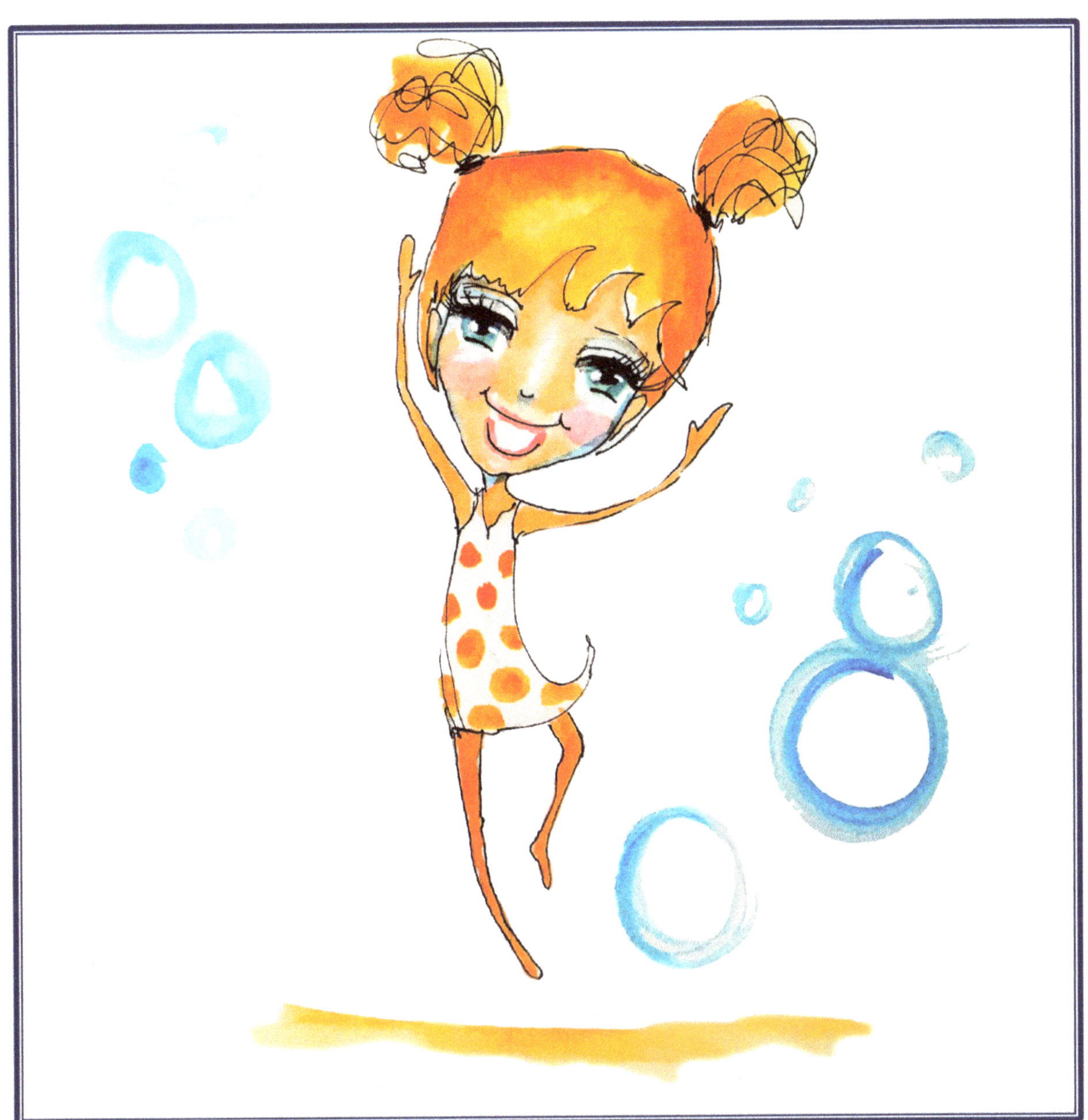

If you would like to see the creative process that inspired this series of books, please go to http://tiny.cc/graceprocess to access a free video I've made as a token of my gratitude to you for joining me along the way.

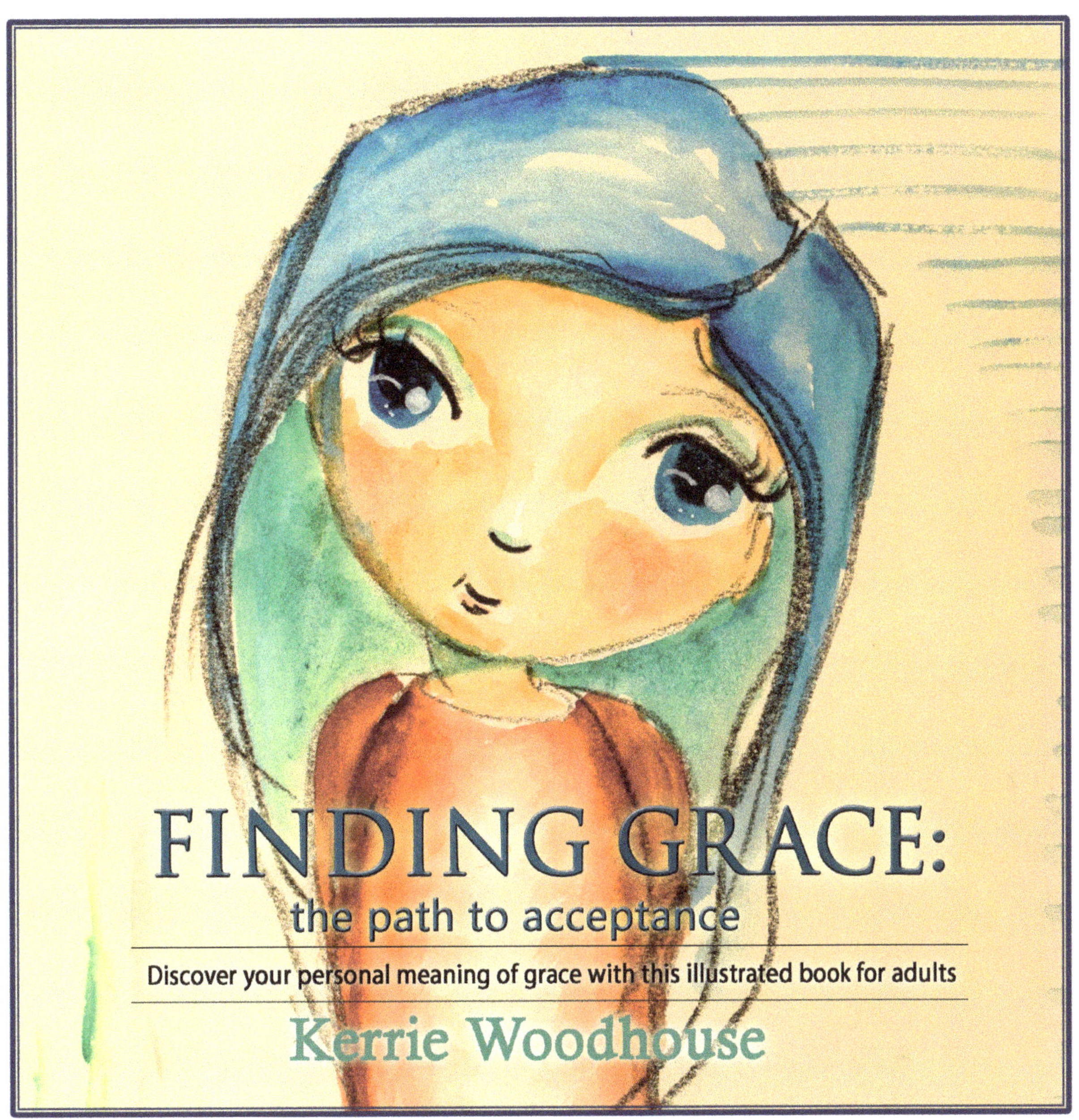

FINDING GRACE:
the path to acceptance
Discover your personal meaning of grace with this illustrated book for adults
Kerrie Woodhouse

If you have enjoyed this book, please leave a review!
You can visit this link to do so: tiny.cc/reviewjoy

Your review will increase the chances of this book
finding its way into the hands of more people like you.

Look out for the other titles in this series:

Finding Grace: the path to acceptance

Embracing Hope: the path to possibility

Keeping Faith: the path to confidence

9 780099 539863 4